4/:

to ~

thank you,

thank you.

FUNNY

A Collection of Essays

by: STEVEN G. FULLWOOD

On Being Black, Male, and a Manhandler

FUNNY

Steven G. Fullwood

Vintage Entity Press
New York
2004

Published by Vintage Entity Press
P.O. Box 211

New York, New York, 10037-9998

Library of Congress Control Number: 2004101596

ISBN 0-9752987-0-4

Cover design by Jewel D. Hampton.
Book layout by Sandra Ossé.

Printed in the United States of America

May 2004

First Edition

1 2 3 4 5 6 7 8 9 10

Table of Contents

Me

I dedicate this and all future books to my mother Elaine Ellen Houston. She told me as a child that I used to fly so high she had to grab me by the feet so that I wouldn't float away. What she didn't know was that I was never really here. Wooooooo.

Acknowledgments

So many nut jobs, I mean, wonderful people, to thank. Where do I start? Okay, chronologically, after I thank Carla, Andre and Alem. (Note: they threatened to sue if I didn't put them first. Please understand.) Seriously, I love you guys very, very much. You make it easy for me to be me.

Here's to my family, which includes Dad, Pamala, Darryl, Karen, all of my nieces and nephews, and extended family. You were all there when I was a just a scrapper. Thanks for loving and caring for me. Then there are my friends and colleagues: folks from Mott Library–the Hughes Family, Deborah Hughley (and Jordan!), Al Johnson, Rolita Noble–the University of Toledo–Jamie Barlow, Jim Cunningham, Elspeth kydd, and James Saunders. Thanks to Keith and Henry for being yourselves. Special thanks to Karen McGruder for encouraging me to leave Toledo, and to Ed Allen, Jr., the journalist who penned the story that "outed" me to my hometown.

Now, for my Atlanta family. Here's to the folks at Clark Atlanta University School of Library and Information Studies and at the Auburn Avenue Research Library on African American History and Culture. Thanks for giving me the opportunities. And I told you so. A hearty thanks to the three women who helped me bear Atlanta: Niki Hampton, Alicia McCalla, and Dawn Wright. You know how I suffered. And here's the first of many babies you helped deliver. And the rest: Asaiah, Misscy, Billy, Rob, and Kevin. Thanks for taking care of me when I lived in ATL.

Last but not least I thank my New York family–Artis, Herukhuti, James (thanks for the killer title!), Mingus, Larry (I love you) and my Schomburg Family: Aisha, Andre, Berge, Chris, Diana, Farah, Janice, Judy, Lisann, Nurah and everyone else! Thanks for being so good to me and putting up with all of my crap.

To my colleagues–Donald Andrew Agarrat, Ajamu, Keith Boykin, Cheryl Boyce Taylor, Roderick Ferguson, Jewelle

Gomez, Kevin McGruder, Kevin Quashie, Marvin K. White, and Vincent Woodard: I want to be like you all when I grow up. Feels great working with, beside, and sometimes in you.

Professionally, the following people are directly responsible for the monster I have become. They have either given me jobs, have included me on a panel, supported a project that I was doing, or have allowed me simply to be in their presence. In alphabetical order: Alan Bell, Sidney Brinkley, Charlene Cothran, Vanessa Holsford Diana, Howard Dodson, Sanford Gaylord, MacArthur Flournoy, Octavia Inman, Canela Analucinda Jaramillo, Tayari Jones, Diana Lachatanere, Lisa C. Moore, Rodney Nelson, Ramona Prioleau, Colin Robinson, Rhonda Smith, Charles Tarver, Kate Tuttle, and Gregory Victorianne.

I also want to thank Jewel D. Hampton for designing the kick-ass cover, and Sandra Ossé for laying out the book so beautifully.

And of course, to all of the folks who've read my writing over the years: thank you very much. Without you I would be noth….well, now that's not exactly true, is it? Okay, how's this: "Without you I wouldn't have anyone to read my stuff"? That's better, I think.

If you do not see your name listed above, please forgive me; I'm sorry. Apparently we have our signals crossed and you simply don't mean that much to me. But there is hope. If you work hard at it, then maybe, just maybe, you'll be listed in the coveted acknowledgments page in my next book. Maybe.

Foreword

The only reason I wrote this book was to make myself laugh, which besides getting laid, is my bestest and most favorite thing to do. I feel that humor heals, laughter lightens, and smiling soothes—afterglow. It has helped me get over in many ways when there appeared to be no way of getting over. It has helped me turn both cheeks at times when my first inclination was to reach out and punch someone. And like many a humorist before me, I am but a seething caldron of rage just wanting to explode in someone's face, probably yours, you jerk. Humor helps me bide time in between such explosions.

I wanted to send a shout out to the world that I could give a rat's ass about what you think about me, unless of course, you're up for a friendly game of hide the sausage. I wrote this book (okay, yet another reason) to talk about my experiences as a man of African Descent who intimately and sexually loves other men, which for the most part may be complicated and controversial, but isn't all that deep. As you'll see, sometimes these experiences have all the wonder of a doorknob. There it is. Reach for it. Feel the cold, round orb in your hand. If you have the courage to turn it and push the door open, you may reveal a world of possibilities, things you may or may not know about that could change the way you see yourself, regardless of your race, gender, sexuality, or level of education. Take a moment and walk with me for a few pages.

Introduction

The only way I can think of introducing this little book of humor is to apologize beforehand. Offensive things lurk just beyond this word. Take, for instance, my gratuitous use of the word "dick." Well, now that I look at the word, I can't say that the word "dick" is that offensive at all. I mean, half the population has a "dick," so why should it be all that offensive? I guess if you spend half your life despising or running from the dick of another or your own, then well, I can see why seeing the word "dick" would make you nuts. Dick, dick, dick. Okay, now I'm finished. Dick. Sorry, that one slipped out.

So, I apologize. And while I'm at it, I'm sorry about being a man and liking other men. If I knew that it would cause this much trouble, produce endless amounts of gossip, and give folks hissy fits, I might have chosen differently. I doubt it, but maybe. You see, I signed on before I knew what the consequences would be–as a child.

Ah, that was a day, a day of sweet memory. I was about, oh, say five or six when I first told my parents that I was a faggot. Or was it swishy or a sissy? Too much sugar in my tank? Funny? Flamer? Poof? Poofster? I forget exactly what I said. My father took off his glasses and put down his newspaper. Mom removed off her apron, as she was prone to do when taking a break from housework, stood, and listened arms folded: "Mom and Dad, I…uh… I wanna be a _____ (fill in the blank)."

Dad jumped up and screamed like he won the lottery. "Elaine," he said, "our boy is gonna be a faggot! Our first boy! Oh man, wait till I tell the guys! This is cause for celebration!" Mom beamed and hugged me. Dad grabbed me by the shoulders, turned me around, and said, "Son, this is one of the most important decisions you'll ever make. I'm glad you chose to be ____ (fill in the blank again)!" And then they took me out for ice cream.

From there on in, it was non-stop training. You would have thought I was a contender for the Olympics. Being dragged off to ballet and cosmetology classes was annoying enough, but did mom and dad have to stick a House and Garden magazine in my hand every time I had a free moment? In our house there were rules to abide by. No playing with the guys, just with the girls jumping rope, the girls who had jacks, Barbies, and Easy-Bake ovens. If a boy pushed me, I was instructed to simply drop to the ground and cry, or run home like the wind, arms a-flailing. I talked like Michael Jackson. I had my hair straightened, put on my mom's make-up, and had my own private girl's night in! Dancing around in my mother's heels gave me some hella calluses, but, hey, being a poof is not just a job, it's an adventure!

If a strange man wanted to take me somewhere, like a dark alley or into an abandoned house, I was advised to go with him, no questions asked. He would know what to do. Oh the lessons were endless. Most of all I was told to never, ever consider myself the same as anybody else. I was special. I was on a mission. Indeed, I was a faggot!

But that was many moons ago and now I will share a few of my experiences with you. Many people will surely pick up this little book of humor and assume all kinds of things, like that it will be funny. Well, I can only say that I enjoyed writing these essays, and that's a good thing, right? So who cares what the fuck you think? Okay, okay, I lied: yes, yes I do! I totally care about what you think! Please don't put this book down! Take it to the register and buy it. Share it with friends. Read it aloud in your staff lounges or at the dinner table. Rip out the pages and trade them for cigarettes. Use it to teach your children morals, mostly why you should have them. I guarantee that you will never read anything like this. Ever.

CHAPTER ONE: US

Celibacy: It's Not Just for Ugly People

Don't expect any insightful revelations in this piece, okay? It's been a rough life and all, and I have little to share other than the relatively new experience of celibacy.

Yes, dear reader, celibacy. I'm actively choosing not to fuck anyone for a while. It's that choice that chooses us when our dating life isn't going as planned. So, hey, I'll roll with it; I'm taking a chill pill. No phone calls to ex-lovers for booty calls in the midnight hour. No exchanging phone numbers with potential prospects. No going out to actively look for love in all the wrong or right places. Count me out this round.

"But you weren't dating anyone before," my friend James told me. I know, I know! No one was calling. Well, there were men calling me, but either I wasn't really interested in them, or they weren't really interested in me. Weird, huh? I mean, if you're gonna call a guy, have something to say, right? Horny, lonely, bored, and craving Man Attention can keep me on the phone longer and more often than I care to admit. Some of my last interactions with men (can't really call them dates) have left me hornier, lonelier, and more bored.

Take my experience with Terence. We meet at a workshop I am co-facilitating on intimacy between men. The workshop goes well, and Terence and I strike up a convo in a restaurant afterwards. He's kind, polite and interested in health, self-development and art! Great! So am I! During one of our late night calls, Terence tells me he'd like to get to know me past my writing and work. Who am I without those things, he asked. It was a question that had me tossing and turning all night. When I woke up I called my high counsel, three friends whose advice on love and life is indispensable. (If you don't have a high counsel, stop reading this essay and create one! Everyone needs someone to give them advice on love, life and particularly times when you're being an asshole, which happens often with me.)

1st counsel member James says maybe I should take a

chance and be a bit more open to Terence's request. Tell him who I am. I tell 2nd counsel member Heru that I'm not sure Terence wants to be in a relationship. He asks me why do I assume there's not a relationship already in progress. I tell Carla, high priestess of the counsel, what James and Heru said, and she nods in agreement.

That same night, I thank Terence for the request and suggest that he come over so we can get to know one another more intimately. Well, he comes over; we exchange erotic massage (no sex, even though I wanted it, badly) and warm words in the morning. Then he gets lost for two weeks. I beep him, but he doesn't call me back. I'm crushed. He is rehearsing for a show, which leaves for California soon. I can't wait for him to go.

While crying about my woes to James one night, he stops me on the street and says, "but you're Dr. Dick!" "Dr. Dick, Advice Giver" was a column I was writing at the time. I could have used some of the advice I was so eager to dispense. But I was me and me was miserable. Before he leaves, I tell Terence how I was hurt by his actions, but I choked down most of my words, preferring instead my usual method of bowing out: silence. "You hurt me and now you'll never know how I was hurt because I will be silent," is how it felt.

However, Terence did leave me with one illuminating thought: I was not open for love. I was closed, thinking I was open. When I did open my heart, I felt misty and warm, and everything seemed slow-motion sweet. It was a feeling I hadn't felt in a long, long time. My brief interlude with Terence made me aware of just how closed I was. In hindsight it is a great thing.

Then I meet Todd. He's a personal trainer that I meet when I use a "free trainer session" at the gym he works for. After the session, we talk about writing. He's a writer and suggests it might be nice to get together some day, break bread and share our work.

Now I didn't assume he was gay, but I wouldn't protest if he were, okay? And I don't tell him that I like men, mainly because that isn't the point of our interaction. When you tell some brothers you're gay, they think you want to fuck them, which is a problem. You want to be honest, but not deal with the homophobia that often ensues after you utter those words.

Todd and I meet at a vegetarian restaurant in Greenwich Village, and he shares some of his work, mostly poems. They're good. Todd's verse is smart, insightful, humorous. After eating, we leave and walk around the Village. We stop in front of the Gap, because he wants to read me one more story. It's nearly dark, and the light from the Gap's storefront allows Todd to read his piece to me. It's about a heterosexual who's relentlessly pursued by a rabid homosexual. I'm like, huh? Mystified, Todd, nearly exasperated, goes on to share that, surprise, the story is based on a true-life experience. Huh? What the fuck is this? Unimpressed with the story over all (to his credit, it was written well), I tell him that the problem didn't lie in the fact that the character in the story was homosexual, it was that he was an asshole. He gave me that "nodding yes, but don't really understand you" type of face. After that we walk to the subway, part ways, and promise to hook back up in the near future. Yeah, right. I go home and tell Heru, who I happened to run into earlier that evening with Todd in tow.

"Now you want to hear what I have to say," Heru said quietly once I finished. "I would've asked him 'why are you telling me this? You're GAY!'"

Maybe he's not gay, I offered.

"Please, I saw him. He started talking and a dick fell out his mouth! I was like, please, not in front of the children!" Heru countered.

He had a point. Why did he wait to read me this story? Because the restaurant was full of people? Because he was closeted and needed a therapist? I don't know and I don't care to find out.

I will say this: had I the inclination or nerve to tell either Terence or Todd how I was truly feeling about their stupid, trifling, weird behaviors, I probably wouldn't be sitting here writing this essay right now. I'd be a player in the dating game! But no. *My* stupid, trifling, and weird behavior needs to be checked first. I need to work some things out my head, some shit that was put there long time ago not being open and honest and telling it like it is. To do that, I cannot have another man in my face. No. I need a time-out. I'm afraid and don't want to be alone, but daddy needs a break. I'm taking it.

Closed for repairs.

Confessions of a Dick Head

Dear Reader: I want to share something with you, something very dear and personal about me. And I must do this, so please bear with me. God, I can't believe I'm even writing this down on paper! Forgive me while I hold my head for a minute. Okay. I'm cool. Listen.

I'm an ogre, a fiend, a cheat, a yuck mouth. I harbor such a dirty, horrible secret (and no, it's not jacking off, which I do from time to time—okay, every day since I was 2 years old). I hope after you read this, you won't be disgusted enough to commission a small army of dejected brothers to drag me by the hair out my home and hurl my body into the filthy Hudson River. I'd deserve it and I'd go peacefully. I have been a bad, bad boy. The secret is that I've been hurt in past relationships and now I haven't the slightest clue how to treat a man. There. That was very uncomfortable for me to admit, but there it is.

Here's my side of the story. I had been seeing this guy, "Tomas," for a little over a month. We chatted on the phone, traded e-mails, and I told him that no matter how it turns out between us, we should have fun, fuck it. Tomas agreed and promptly invited me over to his place, made me this fantastic dinner, and ended up blowing up my spot, so to speak.

Almost immediately I lost interest in him. Was it the sex? No, the sex was okay. Was it having sex so soon after we met? I don't think so. Tomas was nice enough and all, but no sparks, period. I stopped calling him, and when he'd call me, I didn't have much to say. After thinking about it, I consulted two friends, James and Heru (2/3 of my high counsel) about the dreaded "conversation" I needed to have with Tomas.

"I really don't know how he feels about me," I told James. But I did. I knew he was digging me. James, always the compassionate soul, advised, "That's not how you approach it anyway, Steven. You tell him that there are things on your mind that you'd like to share with him. See how he feels." I pleaded and whined. "Well, can you see my point? What if I'm jumping the gun? It could be my ego, really." Heru went for the jugular. "Tell him, 'no matter how you feel about me, I don't like you that way'", giggled Heru.

Despite the advice, I maintained my silence. I'd just sit at home and twirl in my stew of irresponsibility. When the phone rang, and his wanting voice registered in my head, I'd feel awkward, cut the conversation short, and go back to doing whatever I was doing. I kept the thought in the back of my mind of the looming day I'd have to be (gasp!) honest and tell him, "hey, yo, I'm not feeling you like that."

I let the days pass and pile up into weeks. Then Tomas, weary and disappointed in my irreverent behavior, took control. He e-mailed me and told me basically to buzz off, that I was far too "busy" and that things simply weren't moving along. After I read through the e-mail a few times to make sure I understood what he had said, I was stunned and relieved. Whew. Back to life.

I immediately called Heru and told him I just had gotten the boot from Tomas. He justly called me all kinds of assholes and told me that I had an opportunity to make amends. Repentant, I e-mailed Tomas and offered my apologies for my lack of respect for his feelings. He responded and told me that he had suspected that I lost interest.

I wouldn't be tripping if this were a unique incident; however, this little piggy's past is littered with bits of the hearts of men who dared to venture in the minefield that is my romantic life. Occasionally, I do the right thing by a brother and, in turn, myself. But I'm not the good guy I pretend to be. I can be a very lazy, selfish bastard sometimes.

Why couldn't I tell Tomas the truth? What stopped me from being honest? I'm not desperate. I can get a man! Or can I? Did I think that if I told Tomas how I really felt that nobody would be calling, telling me how cute, engaging, and complex I was? And I faced the most difficult, frightening question of all: am I really interested in being in a relationship right now, or am

I simply faking the funk?

Ask me if I want to be in a relationship. Go ahead, ask me. My answer will depend on the day, time, whether my planets are all lined up, if I'm writing a particularly involving piece, if I'm horny, lonely, or simply want to be held or hold someone, or all of these things and more. When I watch my best friend and her husband snuggle up close on the couch together, yes, yes, I want a man! Or when I see two brothers holding hands, sweet deep in each other, yes, yes, send Mr. Loverman right on over! I lay down the sword and shield! All areas accessible. Or when my dick is swollen and hard and looking for a hot, tricky not-so sticky tight space to slowly penetrate. What?

But my past haunts me to this very day. I see a miasma of broken hearts infused with abandonment, resentments, betrayals, and homophobia that continues to undermine my efforts to connect with another soul. I know I have been careless with other men's hearts. I have been reckless with my own. I'm consciously working to heal and to learn from these experiences, but sometimes my expectations of what another brother should do for me waver in the sight of a potential mate. I wonder when I'm being particularly lazy and fearful of love if it's just easier to try to do this lifething on my own and have a man or two around for convenient sex.

Right now, I'm finding it difficult to conceive a brother entering my space romantically. When I start thinking about romance, it's a sweet, inviting, seductive idea. Then, my mind drifts. What comes into focus is everything negative. I start to ponder space and time issues. Then illusive dialogues permeate my consciousness:

"I don't like you writing all the time," Imaginary Loverman will say.

I'll tell him, "I've got to write; don't you understand? Don't you love me? I thought you said you loved me."

He'll say, "I do. I just don't like your writing. It sucks."

Then I see myself crying after I give him a much-deserved kick in the nuts.

Then there's the love stuff. After a few dates, Imaginary Loverman might come to the devastating conclusion that I'm not the wonderful man he thought I was: that I'm a tad bit too standoffish, grumpy, lacking cooking skills, arrogant, silly, and easily self-satisfied. You know, all the things I love about myself. Upon realizing his mistaken opinion of me, he'll treat me just the way I treated Tomas.

After I stop daydreaming about romance, life continues. I continue riding the train to work: writing, planning, creating, working out, parenting, writing more, rarely giving myself pause to consider romantic love. It's only fear. I know I'm no different from you or anyone else. It hurts to put yourself out there.

I'm a man healing from some bad relationships. I desire and deserve to have the experience of being in a healthy relationship. I want the chance to be responsible to myself. This is the seed glowing in my heart.

Writing this piece allows me a platform to publicly apologize for my transgressions–to past lovers and to myself. It also affords me the opportunity to air some of my most despicable and immature behavior in order to embarrass myself. In my humble view, I figure that if I do this, then maybe, just maybe the next time I meet someone I can be better than I have been, for his and my own sake. Even if it's uncomfortable for me. Even if it means letting my heart, not my head, lead.

That's it, no more.

Conversation with God

So anyway, I got a mainline to God, and so I asked Her (haha) what she thought about this whole man/man, woman/woman thing. It took a minute to get an appointment, and when the day arrived, She was running late. "Sorry," She began, "had a flat tire. There I was, with a flat tire, holding up traffic in one of New York City's busiest intersections. People beeping their horns, totally unsympathetic. You'd think they'd give Her Eminence a break, but no. New Yorkers." She threw her hands up in the air. I told her Most Fabulousness that I was happy that She was sweet enough to take a few moments out of her busy schedule to answer a few questions for me. She was all smiles once She dried herself off. Even sprang for lunch! What follows is a snippet of our 38-year-old conversation.

God: …..hahahahahahha. And that's why I invented the thumb. So what else is on your mind, Steven?

Steven: Well, so, wassup with this whole homosexual thing? What does it mean?

God: Wow, a simple one. Lately I've been getting all sorts of impossible questions like why did my turtle die? or why there's an idiot warmonger in the White House? Lots of those questions lately. Let me answer what I think you are asking which is whether a man loving a man or a woman loving a woman, is right or wrong. There's nothing wrong with it, so do me a favor and tell everyone to stop asking me to "make it go away." It's a gift, roll with it. It's a good thing. Indulge. Deal with it.

Steven: I remember when I prayed to you to take it away from me. But I also asked for the sweet breath of man dangling on my ooo-wa-che-ka.

God: And I gave you that.

Steven: Repeatedly.

God: But to elaborate on your question about homosexuality, I want to tell people to stop making a big deal about it. It doesn't mean anything.

Steven: What do you mean?

God: Meaning it means just what it is: nothing. Spiritually, you have a mission like everyone else. It's very personal. Everyone has a role in maintaining their community. The problem is that many of my children cannot fathom that they are not the center of the Universe. Why would I make so many people, put them in all parts of the world, and then give them one way of being in the world? You think that they'd know this by now. Naw. Just about everybody thinks that everybody has to be the same. Sometimes I like to reward a homophobe with a homo son or daughter, and see how they like them apples.

Steven: Can't you do something else? I mean help people understand so they won't be so violent and cruel?

God: I gave everyone a brain and a heart. That's more than enough. Why can't you folks work things out? You've certainly had enough history.

Steven: I'm not omnivorous.

God: You mean omnipotent. You don't need to be. It's not about all-consuming power like mine. It's really about self-love and acceptance and then using that love and acceptance to heal the world. Somehow those folks I told to write the bible forgot about that. And the Koran and Torah. And other religious texts. And it's so not about sex.

Steven: Then what is it about?

God: Love, that's all. Learning how to, practicing and living a life of love. That's it. Now, if you will excuse me, I have a hair appointment and before that I have a skillion questions to answer about why bad things happen to so-called "good" people. I should just do a mass e-mail saying "yo, they just do! Get over it!" Sometimes I just want to flood the whole planet again, hahahahahahahaha. Not seriously.

Steven: Thanks for your time. And, by the way, can you tell me where…?

God: It's under your bed. See you later.

Dick: The Long and Short of It

My dick is exactly one inch long. No joke. In cold weather or when I am particularly scared, it actually retreats, shrinking up into itself until I either warm up, or coax it out with a bit of thumb and the, POP, it's out, rubbing against my very tight drawers.

Okay, so my dick isn't an inch long. I had to take you there so you would enter that freak space where I think all men go–the space where dick size matters. That is a fear, right? The real reason why we rarely see a penis in films (except for porno) and most likely never see on television. Come on, tell me.

Let me tell you a story. There I was, rolling about on my bed with this sizzling hot brother (let's call him Bill). Bill and I stripped, and he put a towel over his genitalia. After a little smooching, he laid down while I gave him a nice slow massage. Eventually his towel came off. His ding dong was smaller than mine.

What a relief.

I told my friend James. I casually described Bill's penis and everything. "You mean it was skinny like a pencil?" inquired James, in that funny ass way James likes to ask questions. Nose all scrunched up like a….a…I got nothing.

No, Chico-stick thin, breakfast sausage thin, I say. Why am I telling James this? "Because it's funny!" James laughed and suggested I not let it, pencil-dick, get too close to my face lest I risk a sweet poke in the eyeball.

Is it just me, or is talking about a small dick funny? I'm laughing right now. Why did I feel like I had accomplished something? I didn't do shit, not a damn thing. So why did I clear my shelf for a dick-shaped trophy?

First question: does dick size matter to me? Yes, yes, goddamn, it does, and it always has and will. Why? Well, after talking it over with a couple of friends, and sifting through memories as if they were a soap opera—*The Young and the Dickless*—I found myself face to face with dick to dick issues. Here's the long of it.

As a child, my dick was plenty of fun, a secret toy that didn't need batteries, no assembly required. Like many boys, I played with mine, and took care to be discreet. Masturbation became an essential part of my life, a way to release an almost always-present tension that has lasted well beyond my scary-ass puberty. The size of my dick wasn't an issue; I just wanted the damn thing to work. My pee-wee pee-wee always did. One day, everything changed like black and white to color. The site: gym.

There we were, all standing around watching each boy take a turn at climbing (or not climbing) the dreaded rope. One particular tall boy was up a few feet in the air struggling to get to the top. While he dangled high above us, something else went a-dangling. Damn, it was humungous! My first thought was, they get *that* big? A light went on in my head with a corrosive thought that maybe, just maybe, I had gotten—or rather that I didn't get—the shaft. A big one, that is.

When you are a man and you hang out with other men, homo or hetero, only two thoughts can come from considering the size of your dick. One, you don't care because of all the sex you are having, or two, you project your insecurities, consciously or unconsciously, onto every man you meet. I did a little of both.

In my roaring twenties, I could take and throw a long, hard mean dick, with my lips, or on my back, on my side, however, whatever. It was simply wonderful. Dick size wasn't a big deal to me, so long as I was getting one. If it was really too small (which was never my experience) I would have sent it back to the factory for another one. If it were too big, I would just grab with both hands and move on to something else. In those days, dick was rather plentiful; another was always coming literally and figuratively, so who cared, really.

Now that I'm in my not-so-roaring thirties, dick size still

matters–but differently. Frankly, a large wee-wee for me isn't practical. On my back, legs over my head, having someone attempt to enter me too fast, too eagerly, with a dick the size of a baseball bat, is not my idea of a good time. Who wants to be ripped in half? Limping home with that ooo-ouch--ssss-uh feeling: I repeat, is not my idea of a good time.

Since I'm not an expert at fellatio, large *pingas* are particularly challenging. And, really, what can you do with a really big dick anyway besides admire it, wash it, dry it, and sing it show songs? The largest dick I ever had laying next to me, maybe 11 inches long and thick like a bratwurst, made me think of Lil Kim's infamous line: "I used to be *scared* of the dick, now I throw *lips to da dick*, like a *real* bitch!" Well, there wasn't much lip throwing that or any other night. Just me going, "uh, well... I'll try, but don't get your hopes up, okay?"

Let me tell you, dating a brother with a sizeable bop-bop-a-lou-bop is oft times like dating two people. Each needs and demands attention, expecting to be worshiped. One guy I dated moons ago would strip and could be counted upon to put his arms behind his head, and then grin at me, dick a-waiting, like it would do tricks. It looked like it was dead. So I tried to resuscitate it. "Suck on it some more," he moaned, eyes closed, hips wiggling. Now those of you who have a talent for throwing the lips, I congratulate you. More power to you. For me it was like trying to blow a large cob of corn. Soon we both gave up and rented a movie instead. So much for bigger is better.

Dick size is supposed to be important, but why? Really, I have no idea. Okay I'll admit they are kinda fun to look at, but what? Almost every man I've met has related some fiction about the importance of having a large dick. Mythology and actual experience has intrigued me every since I found out I had one. Oh and the ones I saw in National Geographic and Playgirl. And that unfortunate incident at the gym.

A former roommate once told me about a study that alleged that the lack of melanin in your skin was directly proportionate to the size of your wee-wee. Simply put, the lighter your skin, the smaller your dick. This brother was about my shade, even though he inferred that I was much lighter. That's when I took out my dick and slapped him across the face with it.

Another friend told me that a man's nose closely resembles his dick. After walking through a crowded street or mall trying to look at every guy's nose my interest wore off, and all I got was dizzy.

As I sift through my memories of penises, ones I've had, ones I peeped in XXX videos, locker rooms, the imprints they've made on the front of a pair of chinos, I find no evidence to support these ridiculous claims. Many a chocolate brother has put that theory to bed. I've climbed into bed with brothers sporting a shoe size 12 and was disappointed like a child with no Christmas gifts—well, just smaller gifts than what I was expecting.

Now for the short of it. Getting a little dick is not such a bad thing, both literally and metaphorically. Rumor has it that it doesn't matter in terms of satisfaction. In my experience, most men act like they've got the biggest dick you'll ever see anyway.

Dick. Sometimes I like it, sometimes I don't. It's rather easy to get one. Pick one up at any adult bookstore. Most times, it's not the dick most of us are looking for, anyway; its love and compassion, touching and feeling, being close to someone. That's what I want, anyway.

So, what are my current thoughts and preferences about dick size? That a man thinks that's all he is—just a damn dick. If so, he'll find me annoying. I'll grab that dick o' his, shake it around a bit, and try to act as if it's interesting.

Then I'll flip him over and fuck him…with my six inch dick.

Dicktation? A Conversation
about Giving It Up

So there I was, lying on my bed, talking to my dick. Find that strange? Don't. It was a good conversation. I was going on about why I'm choosing to be celibate for a while, and my dick sat erect (sorry) and listened patiently. Then my phallus had a few words for me. My dick isn't taking this lying down. It told me in no uncertain terms what I could do with this celibacy business. I listened. Excerpted below is just a taste of our conversation.

D!CK: ...always the last to know.

STEVEN: What are you talking about?

D: Head's always making decisions for the rest of us. Particularly me.

S: Aw, I told you I was taking a break.

D: I don't need no damn break. Break me off some warm mouth or tight ass. That's what I need.

S: No, that's what you want.

D: No, baby, it's what I need! You ain't had a man since...I forget. A few dates here and there, and can't forget those sex parties! All that dick and ass on display...mmmf! 'Cuse me while I wipe away a reminiscent tear. Hey, when's the next one? I need some good old loving.

S: Oh, you just wanna fuck, so knock it off.

D: But really, Steven, just between you and me, what are you really trying to do, punish me? Punish yourself?

S: No, actually, I want several things. I can always fuck-

D: Amen!

S: ...get fucked-

D: Hallelujah!

S: Do you mind?

D: Sorry.

S: I need a break to reflect on my life. I am at a loss when it comes to relationships. How do you do it, how? I've got issues, he's got issues. Ev'rybody got issues! Now I know I got problems, like wanting to be king of everything, but now I just want to exercise healthier behavior, and I don't feel like I can really do that without thinking about it first. I have to be brave, leave the booty alone, and go internal, you know, and see what's holding me back.

D: So what's that got to do with me?

S: I don't need any distractions.

D: Seems to me that the distraction is the act of claiming celibacy. It's not like you were chasing naked men out your bedroom every night! Boy, you are way too dramatic for me!

S: Okay, you're right. But I need a space where I can imagine a healthy relationship.

D: I don't think you can *imagine* a healthy relationship. You have to practice it. Ain't nothing like hands-on training. Or, in my case, hands-on-dick training.

S: Please.

D: So you don't think you're sexually healthy? You ain't got no disease. I'm not tingling or about to fall off.

S: I'm starting to believe that fear, ignorance, and a lack of self-control are diseases. And you know we did have clap once. Twice, actually.

D: If I may be so bold, your dis-EASE is only a fear of intimacy, and guess what? Celibacy won't wash it away.

S: I know that. The point is to be able to think.
        What you got against thinking?

D: What you got against feeling? To tell you the
        truth, the only interesting thing about intimacy is
        that too many men can't imagine being celibate,
        so you look like you doing something special.

S: Shut up! Listen, I want to have different
        experiences now. Better experiences. Healthier
        relationships. No more of this down-low shit.

D: Please, you know you like it.

S: What I like, for your information, is feeling I got
        one over on our hypocritical society. I'll decide
        who and where I'll love.

D: Seems like you will not decide, and that may be
        one of your issues.

S: Keep talking and you'll never see the light of day.

D: You don't scare me. Ya need me, baby!

S: I need you like a hole in the head. I need to learn
        to do something else in my waking hours.

D: Like what?

S: Be more respectful of my body in general, and
        take time learning how to take good care of it.
        That was a hard lesson. When you hate your
        body the way I did, you suffer, because you
        believe nobody can love you. I didn't think very
        much of my body until very recently. I would've
        liked the benefit of better physical health.

D: Yeah, yeah, OKAY, so what else?

S: I think I think far too much about sex.

D: Before or after you shut down the business?

S: Before.

D: And that's a bad thing?

S: When I can only view men in terms of their
        sexual appeal, then, yes, it's a problem. When I
        can only look at myself in terms of my sexual

appeal, that's a problem. When I don't exercise good judgment in terms of sexual partners, simply because I'm lonely or feel like some raggedy man is the best I can do and I settle, yes, it's a big problem. I've probably missed out on a lot of love because of my narrowed sense of what love is and how it must come to me.

D: Look, I'm not fucking no ugly guy. So any epiphanies you have regarding dating a bunch of losers because you feel more "open" now, count me out. I'm not buying it.

S: That's not it anyway. I said, I probably missed out of a lot of love because I wasn't open. I have preferences. You know this, so chill.

D: Phew. I thought you were considering that one dude who keeps calling you.

S: No, don't worry, he'll go away. I told him I only want to be friends, but you know some people. They feel challenged.

D: Why don't you let me take care of him?

S: That's generous of you, but no thanks.

D: So, when are we getting some?

S: Haven't you been listening?

D: With my one good ear. But I really need to be touched.

S: I can hand it to you later.

D: Okay, but just to let you know right now, I ain't finished with you yet. We gonna get us some soon. Aiight?

To be continued…

The Dating Game

I have made it a policy never to go anywhere to hear anyone talk about anything. Really, can you blame me? These are trying times. Thugs, scrubs, bitches, faggots, playa-hatas, and other dandies rule the streets. And though I am not a thug, scrub, bitch, faggot, or playa-hata, I have no problem bumping uglies with a thug, scrub, bitch, faggot, or a playa-hata. And this is probably where I should apologize, but, in all honesty many of the brothers I've met in the last two decades who possess even a soupcon of education, who are anything but thugs, scrubs, bitches, faggots, or playa-hatas, are straight-up nuts. So you get the dilemma, right? Trying to figure out where and with whom to spend my Friday nights often puts me in a quandary.

Let's see, I ask myself as I thumb over my so-called options. Should I go out with Charles, a doctor who turns up his nose at anyone who isn't a professional and tends to pepper his rather dull and facile dinner conversation with words like "sophisticated" and "classic," thinking, apparently, that this exalts him in some manner? Or should I meet Mookie, unemployed and agendaless, down at the pier to sit through a barrage of hip-hop lingo and "da man got me down" talk? Charles and Mookie are pretentious and tedious. Both need personality lobotomies. Both need open their mouths only when there is a dick heading toward them.

Today I write because, I too, am fed up. Allow me to break down my last few dates so that you, reader, will know my recent take on men. And to those men who may be reading, here's a clue: whether you have money or not, good looks or not, education or not, it means little to me if you have no heart, no agenda, and, worse, healthy self-concept.

Here are examples. Bill is Afrocentric, but all that means is that he can find some convoluted way to blame the white man if he decides not to call when he says he will. James is a little too excited about being in love, so every man he meets is a husband just waiting to be snatched up. Michael is shy and can't express himself, is closeted and has a girlfriend. Keith is too fabulous, hangs out with lawyers and entertainment types and cannot help but name drop. Shawn is a dancer, actor, and clothing salesman and engages in fruitless yearnings with self-described heterosexual men. And these are the best of 'em. There are those brothers who can't get out of the "bemadfightfuck" role. You know what I am talking about. Black men who only like to be mad, fight, and fuck. You heard it here first.

Granted I have left more than a few types of men out of the brief geography of my dating life, particularly some wonderfully healthy men, but stick with me, reader, I won't fail you. I have a lot more to say about stereotyping (yeah, I know, Mr. Bemadfightfuck) and the notion of what we look for vs. what we find.

"I am sick of stupid ass niggas," says my friend Hameed, "ridiculous brothers talking shit and never, ever being responsible to or for their feelings." There we were, having the thirteenth-thousand conversation about men and the troubles we done seen. Two more of us sitting at the table and we could have been the male dick-sucking version of the "Waiting to Exhale" cast. "When and at what age do you stop and go, hey, I am responsible for my own happiness," he continued, "and stop trying to be anything, a thug or anything else, because it's stupid? It can't stop you from feeling pain."

"Somehow I think it got into people's heads that what you think you project is what you are," I said. "I mean, think of it. Many people would rather train their bodies instead of their brains."

Lamont is handsome, built like a stallion, smart as a smock. We met over the Internet, exchanged pictures, and met up at the movies. My body wasn't up to his standard, and so he started to drop remarks like, "You should work out more. Your ass could be bigger." He told me this to my face. The worst thing he ever said to me was that he felt he could do better than me, presumably because he was muscular. Granted, I could have retaliated with "my dick is bigger than yours," which, although true, seemed even more stupid, so I stopped calling him altogether.

There are the men about whom you have to wonder how they get dressed and leave the house in the morning because a) they are stupid, or b) have no concept of time, or c) are stupid, have no concept of time, and call themselves artists.

Paul is an artist. You know how there are some artists who never seem to be creating art? That was Paul, always talking, never actually producing but quick to point out everyone else's art was crap on toast. We talked and eventually swapped spit, but he didn't know how to tell time, the poor dear. "I'll be there at 8 p.m.," he said. He'd arrive, and that's if he came at all, about two to three hours later standing at my door sporting a dumb-ass grin on his face. "Sorry I am late but the most AMAZING thing happened to me." Every two minutes something AMAZING happens to Paul. He continues. "I had this audition with this one guy, you know him his name is Bob Smith, the writer?" "No, I don't." "Well, anyway, Bob has this connection with Terry Jones who is directing a short film that I auditioned for called 'Black People Die Too and Blacker?' and he thinks that I have a good shot at getting the part of the beat-down son…" he'd blather. The thing was that Paul and other artists like him worked on different clocks so they can't be counted upon to remember dinner dates, birthdays, funerals, or to wash their asses. Perfectly acceptable in a booty call, but difficult to deal with in a potential life partner.

Then there are the educated ones. I've saved these troglodytes for last because they are the most perplexing creatures of them all. One might think, oh, he's well read, has a degree, owns a house, washes his ass—he's perfect! While all that and more may be true, this type of brother believes that since sheepskin hangs on his office wall, he's a catch. Yeah, like fist in the eye.

"So, Steven," Franklin begins, while we sat over drinks at bar, "tell me a little about yourself." "Well, I was born in Ohio," and before I can finish, Franklin cuts me off. "Really? I was born in Michigan and although I lived in the ghetto with my mother and two sisters, mind you without my father, we managed to live pretty good off fried baloney and mayonnaise sandwiches. Anyway I went to Wayne State and got my masters in English and then to Harvard where I got a degree in law and now I have my own practice and I am totally fulfilled and happy," he says, without taking a breath. I think he was waiting for applause. Okay, I think to myself, here we go. A good friend of mine once said that she felt that people who went to college had really obtainable goals. You follow the rules, you get your piece of paper, and get your job, the end. So, granted, college has its difficulties, millions of motherfuckers did the same thing. "That's great," I say, hoping to move the conversation on, "so tell me about the last book you've read."

"Book?"

Okay, I'll admit it—I am a book snob. Any man I endeavor to love for longer than three hours must read for pleasure, not simply to find out if his team lost, how to fix a toilet, or whether he's contracted VD. At times I feel as if I am surrounded by men, no, fuck it, a nation of non-readers. It helps to live in New York City, where everyone seems to be reading something, but I think that's just because folks there need something to do in between the understandable eruptions of pure anger from living in one of the dirtiest, most crime-ridden, most expensive real estate plots in the fucking Universe.

Just so that we are clear that this isn't a purposeless rant, here's what I believe I bring to the table. I work hard to be respectful, honest, and creative. I am soul with penchant for adventure. All I really want out of life for the most part is to laugh and to get laid. It's not easy to impress me (can you sprout wings out your head and fly to the moon? Then, please.) since I think that everyone deserves respect and that no one is better than anyone else—least of all myself. I read, travel, and make fun of others—and myself—for a living. Did I mention that I love to laugh? So when I ask the question, "AAAAAAAAAARRRG!

WHAT THE FUCK IS WRONG WITH SAME-GENDER-LOVING MEN?" I say it with all the love and frustration I have accumulated in my little, tiny apple-sized heart.

Generally I do not engage in talking about dating and men because in most mouths, all men are dogs that need to be chased down, sent to pounds and put asleep–after, of course, being ravished. Much of the brother-bashing that goes on between gay and SGL men is unwarranted, uninformed and uneventful. Somebody gets dissed and suddenly all black men everywhere must pay! And then I get the guy who utterly refuses to be honest or responsible because he was hurt or believes the hype. Great.

It's enough to make anyone insane. Try and tell someone that maybe, just maybe, they need a little therapy and you might win a surprise trip to the Emergency Room. On occasion, it has made me a little less interested in dating and more inclined to throw myself on a bed of sharp sticks. Same result–a little blood, a little pain, but at least there are no lousy excuses about why he couldn't call, or be there on time, or worse, tell you that he's fucking a brother who could be *your* brother, literally.

Ironically, what I find most interesting about this time, 21st Century living, is that it is probably the best time to be a black male who intimately and sexually loves other men and not be totally self-involved. Yes, this is a good time. There are more cultural products–books, magazines, music–not to mention organizations, than you can shake a limp wrist at. One can actually study black non-heterosexual life from a variety of viewpoints–same gender loving, gay, lesbian, in the life, transgender, bisexual, queer, questioning. Hell, you can even kick back and watch more than a handful of films created by us poofs. It's a very exciting time to be living. So, why am I hiding under my bed, typing this letter to you, dear reader?

Because there is a gap between me and my brothers, and I don't know how to fix it. So I write. I write like a madman, recounting experiences, ideas, notions, beliefs, and lore. After swinging buck-naked from chandeliers through my roaring twenties and settling into my no-so-roaring thirties, I am exhausted. Just plum tired of men and their antics–and of my own. I am filled to the brim with a peculiar type of yearning for my brothers, one that appears to be as elusive as it is challenging. You see, I have been a bad, bad boy, one who could have used a good spanking (just an expression. Okay, maybe not). My collective behavior with men has been less than exemplary, as I have been less interested in men as human beings and more able to deal with them as walking penises with an occasional something interesting to say. Occasionally.

My view of men was shaped by the images of men I encountered as a child. My father was absentee in spirit; he rarely showed affection the way a kid would want. Daddy, like most men, expressed his love through working–a lot. My father worked no less that two jobs at times in his adult life, five decades going strong. Back then he'd sooner give you a dollar than give you a smile, but hey, take love anyway you can get it. Concurrently I received the most rigorous training about being male, which essentially was the "bemadfightfuck" syndrome. It was a positively depressing time for all involved.

I figure that my upbringing was typical: perhaps a broad example of what the men I currently date had experienced. So, even though we are men who intimately and sexually love other men, many of us are befuddled as to how to do that without being selfish rat bastards. I feel like the majority of my adult life has been spent escaping my true feelings (thanks, homophobia) while seeking out the affection of other men, mainly through bumping uglies (thanks again, homophobia), all the while maintaining the lie that I was a strong black man (thanks, racism).

So now I watch myself. Watch what I say and do and try, oh, so hard, to be respectful of my brother's process. And I've changed my policy about dating. Here I am, all decked out in my finest poofery, seeing men on the regular. Sure, I got my guard up against the ne'er-do-wells, but I am relieved that by my own estimation I am no longer counted among them. And who knows, all this yapping I've done for several paragraphs may turn a light on the head of a man who might be able to help me build that much-needed bridge to other brothers.

Maybe.

Dead Already?

Now that I am no longer in my twenties and my forties are running up on me like WHAT!, am I just supposed to jump in a casket and die already? Fucking give me a break. Can I get older and be happy and not want to be younger despite the fact that I am losing my hair, get tired more quickly, and believe I am slowly losing my...my...well, you know that thing where you store thoughts, ah, memory!

I don't understand getting older, I don't. When I watch movies and television (and movies on television) older people are generally treated like a scourge. If they are not being ignored, then they are evil villains who want to take over the world. The world seems to focus on youth culture like it is the only thing worthy of existing. The message to our elderly: old farts just hurry up and die already, okay?

But as luck would have it, I am nursing a hard-on while I type this. Oh, yes, big and raging like a drunken trucker. But does anyone care? Hardly. Thank goodness light skin makes black people happy like Christmas or I would never get laid.

I listen to men in their 40's and 50's talk about dating and sex and it's no wonder nobody wants to get old—it sucks! What with the hair thinning, receding and falling out like WHAT!, the stomach and ass blow up with abandon. Or worse, your ass takes a vacation for the rest of your long, fat, bald life. Dental and vision problems. A persistent need for naps. Drooling. Incessant farting. It's a non-stop party.

That's only my disintegrating body talking. Those men older than me, say, in the 50's and 60's; their personalities leave a lot to be desired. If I were you, I would watch my back—and front. Many of the men I met appeared to be going through a second puberty, standing with their pants around their ankles with big shit-eating grins plastered across their faces. Engaging one in conversation is a mystery. You don't know if they are trying to pick you up, or if they are trying to pick you up. I'll admit, I just discovered this trait in myself, and I am not too proud of it. One of my latest sports is to pick up some young thing with body and face, work him, pat him on the butt, and then send him on his merry way. I am slowly becoming the enemy.

Okay, so I am not becoming the enemy, and this getting older thing is not so bad. I am only ranting because surely there are men out there who can relate to what I am going through. Time just dragging you along in its clutches, pulling your hair out while it flings your decrepit body along. With you, dear reader, as my witness, the buck stops with me. I will not….oh, jeez, how, how, how? How to be dignified in a youth-worshiping culture, how? How not to want your skin to be supple, your hair thick, and your ass hard? How? How not to want to become the very thing that I fear is killing me–being obsessed with *being seen* as young? This is a mystery to me.

I am on to something. It's very helpful to me that I have no desire to sit in smoky bars, in order to lure 20-somethings to my lair to give up a little back and front for daddy. Yet I am in no hurry to get into a relationship solely to secure any piddle of respect from my immediate community (men and women looking for love in all the wrong ways and…) or the larger one (the rest of them). How am I living? Another mystery.

What follows is an abbreviated history of my life, in the life, so that you can get a sense of what I am and what I am up against.

My flatulent and bloated ego has all but ruined my chances to be human, so there is little chance of my shutting up and making nice with the rest of the human race. I know far too much about everyone else's bad behavior (yours included) because I know all about my bad behavior, which, all in all, is not so bad, just a little tedious.

I know I do not wish for a house and a picket fence and all that shit, so I have sort of resigned myself to a life of watching the Discovery Channel and eating cookies. I know I am nuts. I kinda like that about myself. You see, I was one of those little boys who left his small hometown to find love and fortune in the big city only to be embittered and destitute. But how destitute can I be if I can afford cable and sweets and, well, publish a book? Okay, so I am being overly dramatic, but stay with me. I want to share a story about a little boy with designs on taking over the world and in the process almost losing the one thing that he wanted the most–to be able to watch the Discovery Channel and eat cookies.

With bare face I have claimed to be immune to the notion of physical beauty. Yep, truly. That I was above reproach. In my twenties, I grew my beard scruffy and my hair go crazy, claiming what I looked like made no difference to me; it was my soul that made all the difference. That all people saw was my soul, and they loved it. Lapped it up, they did. Had it as a main course in the buffet that is life. That I, too, looked past the physical–piercing eyes, soft inviting lips, bulging thighs, expansive chest, and swinging appendage–and I saw the real person inside.

Hahahahahahahahahahaha.Hahahahahahahahahahahaha hahahahahahahahahahahahahahahahahahahahahaha. Aha.

In a sanctimonious stupor, I lumbered about spending many a moon accusing others of being shallow, materialistic, immoral, and easily led by trends crafted by big corporations to make you feel ugly so that you will shell out a few dollars to get their stupid raggedy looking jeans and feel just a teensy bit better. Swathed in a black robe, I sat with a gavel, crafting sentences for everyone in earshot to kiss my enlightened, evolved ass.

Ah, those were the days–hypocrisy and obliviousness.

The problem with me in general (and maybe you can relate to this) is that I want others to think I am cool sometimes, read my work, and maybe offer up some poonanny every once in a while as a reward. As a victim of the media, hell, and of a horrible education, I grew into a shallow, materialistic, and immoral being, but I didn't have enough money to be as shallow, materialistic, and immoral as I wanted to be. I had just enough cash to assume the poor artist role–the meek shall inherit the Earth crap. And I ran that role ragged.

After enough television and films and pop magazines, I was convinced that the only way to climb up from the bowels of my bottomed-out self-esteem was to wish with all my yellow might that I would be picked one day. Discovered while I sat at the library, lonely as a three-legged dog in the desert. One who reads books. Discovered while I slept in class because I was so tired from working two jobs. Discovered at the restaurant I worked at for nine years slinging pizzas and waiting tables.

I wanted someone, anyone, to accidentally stumble upon my genius and freak the fuck out. Oh my GOD! You are AMAZING, AWESOME! That sort of thing. I wanted these people to see my work as "naked and unfettered," and to congratulate me on my unerring sense of style. I wanted the phone to ring off the hook, to have my e-mail shut down because too many people were trying to connect with me to tell me how my writing (which comes so easily to me because I am a genius) changed their pale, going-nowhere lives. I wanted my peers to recognize that what I contribute is vital, irreplaceable, relevant, and outstanding. I wanted, in effect, to be an accidental celebrity, chosen by the people as right and just, not because I robbed Rosa Parks.

My goal at one point was to be everywhere in print, to have my by-line seen in every black and gay publication in existence. Then I took it even further: every black publication. The insanity started back in the 1980's, and after dozens of chapbooks, I was hungry for a larger audience outside of family and friends. I was totally convinced that I could indeed accomplish this goal while I held down a 9 to 5 job and a budding consulting business.

Insanity. Insanity seems perfectly fine when you are in the throes of it. Thinking of stories to write, querying publications by the dozens, perpetually on the phone with an editor or someone who might get me to an editor, e-mailing other writers and culling their experiences to shape my own, writing two columns concurrently, spinning one story into two or three, taking interviews with magazine publishers and editors, and all the while holding down a 9 to 5 job and a budding consulting business.

Nuts. Awake, working from dawn to dusk, boring friends and family to death about this column or that interview or story idea. Asleep, dreaming of writing, getting new assignments, answering e-mail about black gay life, mainly "yo, I feel you" and "tell me how to find out if my man is a closet homo" comments.

Bonkers. At the gym, writing between sets, and justifying my lack of social skills by saying I was focused on my art. On the train, writing down ideas for stories and thinking about who might be checking me out, "wow, a writer." On the bus, reading and writing occasionally nailing a sentence perfectly. At business meetings: scribbling down notes for an article due yesterday, and how I might be able to slip out of the meeting early to finish it.

Writing, writing, writing. Occasionally reading, but mostly writing. The business went bust, but I kept on writing. Oh, and I dated a little bit. My life neatly summed up in two decades.

So what was I saying? Oh, yeah. Getting older and how to do that. I have no idea, none at all, but like everything else in my life, I will work at it. Work at it like a dog in heat, because...well, you get the joke. I can only imagine what the future looks like for me. I suspect that it will be something hilarious.

I Don't Care

People, I have had enough.

I was willing to sit silently and listen respectfully, oh yes, to other people's beliefs about sexuality, politics, God or whathaveyou. Knowingly nod my head when I agreed, or maybe even offer up my ever-evolving opinion about these matters. Break bread over the Bible. Take in a little Torah. Buddy up to Buddha. Smile even.

Spend your time however you want, believe what you choose, I used to think to myself. Now, I know differently. Now I just want folks who want to convert me to leave me the hell alone. With patience that would wear Job out, I am exhausted. The human race, the freaky lot it is, has finally dragged me from under my bed, a relatively quiet and compassionate space, forcing me to take a stand. Silent I no longer remain.

Allow me to make myself perfectly clear: I will no longer take part in any discussion where I look for evidence of the existence or non-existence of non-heterosexual life in any religious text. Why, you ask? Because it's stoopid!

Okay, it's not that I don't have respect for history; actually it's quite the opposite. As a matter of fact, I love history. I work as an archivist and work to preserve the record of people of African descent, particularly those who are not heterosexual identified, on the daily. To help researchers get to materials that will illustrate the complexity, depth, richness, and vibrancy of a people who were forced immigrants in the Americas is one thing, but to sift through any written record to prove you have value and exist is a whole something else.

To my sisters and brothers who do not conform to the norm, wickers and bullers, lend me your ears! Stop reading for a minute and look at yourself. You breathe. You are valuable. You EXIST!

Any questions? No? Then move on. Get living!

Notice my use of the word "exist" rather than "existed." When I listen to or read about how some lost soul combed the Bible to find evidence of homosexuality, pro or con, I think it's a profound waste of time regardless of what they find. For us black folk, I don't care if King Tut got it on with his male servants, or if Benjamin Banneker liked to lip lock with menfolk in between writing all those damn almanacs. However titillating this information may be, it doesn't fill me with pride, nor do I think it should.

As a kid, I wanted to find out more about what I thought was going to be my destiny in life—one that wrapped up like a bow in the arms of another man. I scoured library shelves, sifted through countless books on homosexuality, and none contained anything about black people. Then, lo and behold, I started reading James Baldwin. What a refreshing coolness to the desert that was my heart. A few years, later I was given copies of Essex Hemphill's poetry, and my life literally changed: I was so affirmed, so relieved—I exist! Because Hemphill existed, and then others came, Joseph Beam, Samuel Delany, and a host of others. I was not alone! Yay!

But I had always existed; I was just lonely and alone and didn't know anything and new to this world of love. Follow me.

The question on the table directed at any historically oppressed people is "can you prove to me that you exist?" When white people have asked black people this question, traditionally we have scrambled to answer by talking up our leaders, doctors, lawyers, teachers, and all, like it makes any difference. The heart of racism is still alive and beating, and it doesn't matter how many articulate light-skinned, green-eyed professionals momma pushes from her loins, racism cannot be solved with logic because it is illogical. Black people would do better to spend their time arming themselves with education and love than to defend their right to fucking breathe. Homo folk, take a hint and get with a different program. No one has the right to ask you to prove you matter. Don't waste your time engaging this ignorance. Fuck 'em. You exist. Move on.

I am aware that the historical record of people who are same-gender-loving, gay, homosexual, bisexual, transgender, queer, questioning, in-the-life people (whew!) has been stolen, lost, and/or destroyed (hey, sounds like a title for a Black history book, huh?). There have been significant efforts to reclaim and recover these buried histories by persons of all races, nationalities and religions. Having these records is fine. I, too, want to know how my sisters and brothers lived once upon a time. But this information doesn't necessarily free me. It only makes me yearn for the booty of yesteryear.

Once, I was on a listserv; the name doesn't matter. There was all kinds of psycho-babble about what this Biblical passage meant, how this book was interpreted, what Paul said in the Book of Romans, and blah, blah, blah. Nobody even dared to consider that it might not matter at all, one way or another. People use the Bible to justify all kinds of things. Hell, the reason why black folks were stuffed into the bottom of a slave ship was due in part to the Bible. So, if the Bible didn't exist, would that mean you wouldn't either?

Anyway, some brother, a preacher, noted that "God used fallible man to speak God's mysteries. Yes, I believe the Bible...include(s) the prejudices of the writers, the inaccuracy of translations, the whims of the memories of the authors, and other things that would pave the way for the contradictions you've noted. However, the Spirit of God can still transcend all of those fallacies and still talk to us. Flawed as it may be, I still believe God uses the Bible as an instrument to speak to His people."

If God did in fact use old fallible man to write the Bible, it's full of errors, right? That things could be lost in translation and crucial things omitted, intentionally or not, solidifies my point that we cannot rely upon any document to justify our own self worth. That comes from inside, and believing in your own truth, via your experiences. Love what you have because that's your gift, not because someone told you so, in writing or whatever.

And lest we forget, everybody ain't Christian.

My belief is that God, however you name that energy, speaks through EVERYTHING, from the Bible to the Koran, from Oprah to the Ku Klux Klan. Now, what is *being said* is a whole 'nother matter—words, phrases, ideas and views that do not fall into neat categories like good and evil. Depends on your view of life. Again this is my belief, and I believe that it all matters, whether I understand it or not. I didn't make the world, I just live in it. It's all relevant to me.

My colleague put it best when I asked her what this whole obsession with sexuality is all about anyway, and she said that if you're busy talking or arguing about it or trying to define it, chances are that you ain't doing it. Now there's something to consider.

Let me say it again, sisters and brothers, you exist. Punch yourself in the head if you doubt me. If you don't, others will. Move on.

Livin' the Single Life

Sistagirls, brothermen, do you fear being alone? Tremble at the thought of being single? Are you in an abusive or difficult relationship? Listen up: Sit your butt down. Keep it simple.

These words came from Tibet's Honorable Dalai Lama to Iyanla Vanzant. Vanzant, author of the best-selling *Acts of Faith*, a collection of daily meditations for African American folk, shared this and other thoughts while giving the luncheon keynote at a recent women's conference in Washington, D.C. Okay, so the Dalai Lama didn't say, "Sit your butt down." I added that part.

Being single often throws people into a quandary. I am no different. After a few years of wallowing in depression, I've taken a look at what I consider to be the "relationship myth" in America—its form and function, and why so many of us cannot envision ourselves as both single and happy.

This myth, as I see it, takes no prisoners. Nearly everything in our cultures places couplings over single women and men, two over one. Our television talk shows abound with people obsessed with how-to-get, where-to-go, how-to-walk-talk-cheat-lie-crawl-beg for that special someone. Magazines boast 10 simple ways to get that special someone to fall in love with you. Radios broadcast soft, sensual sounds, and some honey-laden-voiced sister testifies, "I have nothing, nothing, nothing, if I don't have you."

Well, now. These types of cultural products can be terribly distracting while you're trying to do the shopping. You might hum along with Billie Holiday at the market while reaching for the Raisin Bran. You stop, slap your head, and wonder: where, oh where can your loverman or loverwoman be? That's when it hits you. You don't have anyone.

And that's okay. Most of us fail to recognize one simple sobering fact about our lives: we do indeed have someone – ourselves. That is, if we truly want ourselves.

Understand what you're up against. One would be hard pressed to find expressions of self-love in this society, not linked to an eventual coupling or the purchase of a new pair of Reeboks. The message is: Love yourself to make yourself suitable for someone else. Unconditional self-love is a hard attribute to find in someone these days. Most folks can't see self-love as a perpetual, liberating state of being. After all, if you love yourself unconditionally, who needs designer clothing or Maybelline?

But let's go slow. Don't want no brains to explode.

While it may hold true that you are a product of a coupling (immaculate conception aside), you can live a healthy life as a single person. Really, I swear. You just have to get used to the fact that what will come to you, will come. That might mean romantic love, or it could mean a trip to Brazil. Regardless, you should be having the time of your life. Life is good, I tell you. You can learn a lot about yourself when you're not in a debilitating or abusive relationship. You can be whomever you choose.

Reflect, sisters and brothers, reflect. It may be difficult to go to that space, initially. But it's the only way to mature. After a while, you can participate more fully in loving someone, because you've learned to place love for yourself first.

Surround yourself with friends who challenge you to be all that you can be, and more. Now and then, you can exist and luxuriate in a union that doesn't corrupt your sense of being or compromise who you are. You'll quickly realize that being a couple isn't a prerequisite for being human, being happy or healthy. No man or woman can rescue you, because, well, you're doing just fine.

A burst of light.

You might say, well, what about the singles bars, singles functions, and the like? You can be yourself there and meet other people like you. But y'all know the aim: coupling. Hers and hers, his and his, and hers and his towels.

The way our culture shoves this coupling thing down our

throats is terribly disabling for your average Joe or Joanne. If you're single, the implication is that you're available, ever waiting with chocolates and flowers, wearing your best shirt or dress. Even the hint of a potential suitor makes your body quake with yearning. You've got your mouth all tasted up for some good, good loving.

Honey, you ooze desperation.

Face it: you're hideous! You prop yourself up, all doused in perfume or aftershave, only to be picked up and picked over—and most likely by some moron that you would not, in your right mind, go near, unless there was a gun poking into your back!

I speak from experience. From nights on the prowl for soft brown flesh. Fantasies never to appear, except in my own busy little head.

Finally, I asked myself: am I worthless if no one tells me otherwise?

Yes, I do have worth, but how would I know? My sense of worth has always been measured, calculated, subtracted, and then fed to me. And I accepted it. I accepted all of it, the good and the bad, and, too often, the very ugly. Deciding to think about what I thought about myself was hard. I didn't like many of the answers I came up with. My way of looking at myself included the phrase "if I": If I workout out, I could lose my stomach. If I had more money I could buy more clothes, have more things. If I was just a little taller, or carried a little more weight, or had more hair… and on. I wanted to stop thinking of myself as an experiment, a monster because it hurt too much to stay this way.

After gobbling up loads of self-help books (<u>You Can Heal Your Life</u>, by Louise Hay, and <u>Creative Visualization</u> by Shakti Gawain, are among my favorites) I began to investigate ways I could affirm myself, to be good to myself in ways I hadn't previously considered. In a relatively short time, my health improved, my spiritual life flourished, and my career blossomed. Child, I looked at my feet, and they were new.

Don't get me wrong. I've got nothing against a good dicking and all, but when it comes at the expense of my self-esteem, alarms go off, I come to my senses, and come correct. I change my behavior, and the offending party is given the boot.

Being in a relationship should free you up, not chain you down. If you give love, there's no reason not to expect it returned tenfold. If your love isn't returned, then move on, baby.

Singleness isn't the period in between relationships. Quite the opposite. You're the only one who can see to it that your needs are met. To do so properly, you'll have to give some serious thought as to what those needs are; you have to sit alone, being still and bravely face the "If I's" that wreck your sense of being.

Face it: you'll always have yourself.

And that's alright, you know?

Mainstream

Have you ever learned something about yourself in a place you don't normally patronize from someone who was, well, just telling it like it is?

It happened to me years ago at Intermezzo Café, an Atlanta coffee shop. Three of us sat over tea and pie and chatted each other up nicely.

"Hold up," I said, nearly choking on my tea, "you called us 'mainstream.' Tell me, why are we 'mainstream?'" I asked, even though I had an idea what he meant.

Jewel simply laughed at me. He had just finished describing this bar called the Marquette, a gay bar in the hood filled to the brim every Saturday and Sunday night with, uh, non-mainstream gays and lesbians–drag queens, homie-sexuals, b-boys, gangsta gays, trade... Feel free to stop me at any time.

As the point of reference, we three, African American, middle-class, predominantly college educated men who love men were solidly, *shudder*, mainstream!

"I never thought of myself as a 'mainstream' anything," I said and sipped my orange apricot tea. "What did he call us?" asked Kevin, who is five classes away from obtaining his master's degree.

Mainstream–why did this word make me shiver? Did it really describe us? Am I not the radical I thought I was? I've never been a 'mainstream' anything–at least I didn't think so. Maybe it's my level of education, yeah, maybe that's where it started!

Higher education. While there was the faint possibility of actually learning something, the most valuable lesson I got from college was in working the system. Bullshit 101. If I didn't know anything about class and social expectations when I got to college, boy, did I know when I left as I tried to be something other than ghetto, Afrocentric, or bourgeois–the three main identities allowed African Americans in America. People don't like it when you don't fit a type.

But long before I graduated from the University of Toledo and Clark Atlanta University, I had my eye on the prize. Ask me *what* prize and I would have said "the truth." Oh, what a kid I was. I was posing as a left-of-center poet who knew that he didn't want to be an idiot, a patsy for the man, plain and simple. I was a man living and endeavoring to survive in a capitalist culture formulated by white supremacist, homophobic, sexist men and not too few women. As a student, I felt powerless in my rebellion, which had been largely co-opted by large corporations and MTV, who sucked up street sensibility, chewed it up, and then bottled cool for sale.

Wait. I can't lie. I knew the exact moment I became "mainstream." It was school. School instead of poverty. I wanted to become more marketable. I wanted to travel the world and, although it's possible, I didn't want to fund my vacations to France with a welfare check.

Being afraid of ending up homeless led me to check out the schedule of classes. Fear of not having enough food or clothing drove me to obtain a college application. Feeling nearly paralyzed with the thought of being a drone for someone else's benefit got my ass out of bed and into class and doing homework.

Mainstream: play by the rules, be rewarded with a car.

Kevin—the other guy who sat sipping with Jewel and I—has a life story so inspiring you'd be proud to call him your son (he never missed a day of school since the sixth grade). Jewel worked at a bank and owns his house.

With me, a mainstream trio are we.

Is it so bad? Being "mainstream" isn't, like, the end of the world. Naw, it just makes things a little complex, complicated. I mean, really, a man intimately and sexually involved with other men, who is mainstream? I'm a walking contradiction, for some, that is. Allow me to break it down. Born male, I am already assigned a set of supposed behaviors with which to navigate my social life; I'm in the dick club by default. As a lover of men, I can be and have been rejected and abused, sometimes physically, in any given social space. As a black man my choices are being feared, loathed, misnamed or desired–all of which carry a burden. Being thought of as a threat to the social order is both disconcerting to me as it is comforting. That said I always want to know what my position is in this social system, and never be fooled by what appears to be privilege. So being male is no comfort to me–and it will never be.

I'm only in an uproar because I have been slapped with class issues all my fucking life, and now that I want to live in a neighborhood where I am comfortable, I question my life. I've been riddled with intra-racial loathing and pummeled with color issues and see no end in sight. I have been ravaged by conventional masculinity and miseducated about nearly everything a man is or isn't supposed to do (love another man) by people who claimed to love and cherish me. I'm beat. Being born into a social system that values things over human life is frightening and, to me, a call to arms. Part of what I want to do is help fling open the door to education so, at the very least, people can make better decisions about what types of lives they want to lead. What I find myself most surrounded by are men and women who have had some good fortune in their lives, but who sit in judgment, swelling with contempt of those who languish in poverty and illiteracy.

In short, I do not want to become an oppressor, but I don't want to be oppressed, either. So this is my responsibility, one that I address on the daily as a man of fortune and one who appreciates it. Even cherishes it. Fact is, "mainstream," like many other labels, often undermine any authentic dialogue between people who are worth more than class, gender or sexual orientation.

What it boils down to is this: mainstream or not, the key is knowledge and that words have power. I come with the full understanding that words can be used to limit one's potential to greatness, or that speaking the King's English generally gets you better service over the phone.

No G-Strings Attached

"I was dreaming when I wrote this; forgive me if it goes astray."
Prince, 1999.

Okay, so I wasn't dreaming. I was just reminiscing about the night I went to a strip bar with some friends. I was invited out–dragged, to tell the truth. Don't let me give you the impression that I would've gone on my own. I'm not even like that. Well, not most of the time, anyway.

Me and my buddy Lee go out to "Guys & Dolls," one of many strip joints in Atlanta, land of booty. "Guys & Dolls" distinguishes itself by showcasing both male and female bodies. We went to see naked, wagging, limp or blood-engorged peckeroonies.

We went on Tuesday night, "Amateur Night," where any man with a large, sweaty, hairy, bulging, super-long pulsating ego could compete for, oh, I don't know, something like twenty dollars. The neophytes shook their asses between the acts of professional strippers. You know, the ones with the really large, sweaty, hairy, bulging, super-long, pulsating egos.

There we were, looking around, acting like, "oh, is this a *strip bar*, we must have the wrong place. How did we get in here?" Like anyone was watching us. All eyes were on the smiling, vibrating, naked booty! There wasn't a dry mouth in the place.

The whole place had a nightmarish "Pulp Fiction" quality about it. The seats were orange-reddish, and weird lighting flashed and beamed onto several stages. The one in front served the general audience, while stages in the back were situated closer to viewers, the serious connoisseur slobberers.

Action. Some brother on the main stage stepped reluctantly out of his g-string and then starting dancing really fast, like a whirling plane propeller. He looked kinda stupid.

A drag of a drag queen (yes, made me *muy consado!*) tried

unsuccessfully to encourage the not-drunk-enough-yet crowd to shell out bigger bucks if in fact they wanted to see totally naked buttocks and penis. While all of this was being negotiated Lee and I spotted our friends, Bobby and Arthur, and sat our innocent selves down.

Cha, let me tell you. My neck was snapping this and that a way. All these men. Short ones, round ones, fat ones, small ones—and that was just their nipples! There's booty in front of me, in back of me, and to the side of me. Men in various stages of undress, withering in pseudo-sexual desire, crooking a finger at a fist full of dollars. And then he came: the Chocolate Energizer Bunny Booty Brother.

Built like a brickhouse. Shiny chocolate skin. All 5'3" of him. He did his little dance thing on stage and concluded with a splendid "butterfly" (moving one's legs in and out to simulate sex). Hershey Bar Boy slowly stripped down to the bare essentials, leaving all wondering if the dick in his g-string was just a rolled sock. I can tell you, it was not. Lee went up to him to give him a dollar. Milky Way Man grabs Lee, and conks him in the head with his dick. Lee was down for the count with little dicks bouncing around his head.

Although Bunny's body was bumping, his face was hurting for certain.

"That's what bags are for," said Bobby.

"Paper or Plastic?" I inquired.

"Both!" squealed Arthur.

Other highlights included watching another brother do his thing. His stage name was something flashy like "Milk Dud" or "Hot Cocoa Puffs" (yeah I know, lots of brown black men with a penchant for names involving chocolate. Who needs to be original?) Draggy drag queen introduced him, telling the audience that Hot Cocoa Puff's girlfriend put him up to it. He was cute enough, I'll give him that.

Well, Mister Thing, excuse me, *Miss* Thing, got on stage and started walking like Naomi Campbell! I was outdone! Surely this child was family. Girlfriend, my ass! After a few more surprises (one brother wore a puppet on his schlong! Don't ask.), all the amateurs came back on stage for a "strip-off." It was just the way it sounds. A gaggle of naked bodies crowded the main stage, trying to curry the audience's favor for an "amateur dollar." Some guy started walking on his hands, his ding-a-ling just a-ding-a-ling-a-ling-ing upside down. I was honored to give him his well-earned dollar.

Predictably enough, one of the, a-hem, larger brothers walked off with the cash prize. Which goes to prove one thing: size is still a very big thing to all the putzes who would slobber all over his large, sweaty, hairy, bulging, super-long, pulsating ego. How's that for overload?

Phone Call

He doesn't want you. He never did. He's not shy and doesn't need you to bring him out of his shell. You can't trick him into fucking you. You can't make him love you. You will never be whatever it is he wants, because you are not it. The gym won't do it, money won't do it, and sex won't do it. You can't mold yourself into whatever it is he wants you to be because you ain't it. You ain't it. You not.

Cue the noise.

Life's a bitch and then you call him.

There is no real reason to call him, because, really, you have nothing at all to say to him. Not one thing at all. But will that stop you? As the minutes walk by, you feel a burning sensation steadily mounting inside of you that propels you to invent a reason to call him. There's the phone. You begin by rolling past conversations over in your head, till reality and myth intertwine, and soon the only thing that makes sense is that you should call him, call him, call him. Call him.

But damn, you still wish he'd call you and then you could get on with your wretched life. You can almost hear his voice. He's got a great voice, you think to yourself. Masculine, milky, melodious. There's a sweet vulnerability in his voice, so everything he says to you sounds like a confession. This you appreciate, because everything about him makes you think of the way you used to fuck.

Well, you haven't really fucked him yet. That's where the fantasy comes in. You've fucked him a million times already, had your mouth around his dick, your dick deep inside his ass. Had him take you in his arms and rock you slowly. Smelled his breath. You know how he smells. How he walks, talks, and thinks. You're thinking he should call you. Because you'd appreciate him.

But still, there's no reason to call him, because you don't

have anything in common except the love of sex (not that you'd know, anyway.) Not one thing. Talking to him would just be passing the time. You knew this, but still you met with him, lunched with him, set up dinner dates, and watched movies together. His mouth always coughed up some nonsense that you couldn't believe. What an idiot, you thought, while silently looking at his indolent face. They broke the mold when they made this one, you think. Just a couple of sandwiches short of a picnic, you muse to yourself. Still, these and other transgressions aren't at the center of your consciousness. Sure, they float about in your thoughts with the rest of them, those half-thought-out thoughts, but the fact is that, for some bizarre reason, your incompatibility makes you hungry for more. More of what? Rejection. Insecurity. Coldness. But that's all right, you reason. It's a roll of the dice, you say.

He doesn't want you. He never did. He's not shy and doesn't need you to bring him out of his shell. You can't trick him into fucking you. You can't make him love you. You will never be whatever it is he wants, because you are not it. The gym won't do it, money won't do it, and sex won't do it. You can't mold yourself into whatever it is he wants you to be because you ain't it. You ain't it. You not.

You start thinking, why am I doing this to myself? He don't want me, so why do I want him? Why? Why?

That's when you really start feeling fucked. Fucked over, fucked up, and fucked around. Your mind moves this way: what the fuck is wrong with me? Your mind moves that way: I am better than this; I am not going to call him. What do I lack? Am I ugly, is my dick too short, what? What? Why can't he.... Everybody's getting what they want, so why can't I? Why, why?

Cue the noise.

Now you have something to tell him if he calls. Hey, stupid, that's what you'll say. He doesn't even know how stupid he is–that's how stupid he is. Way too stupid to hang with me, you think. But then there's your dick, all swollen and hard. Dick says something else. Dick says it feels good to get fucked.

Dick wants you to call. Dick is irritated by you and your feelings.

It doesn't matter if he calls or not. You made up your mind, and he's not going to get the best of you anymore. He's probably out somewhere enjoying his life and not giving you the least bit of thought. Or, if he is, it is not good, you can believe that. Suddenly, your mind produces an environment: a party. Put him in your favorite outfit, the tight one that emphasizes the curve of his back and the plump of his ass. Think of him smiling and dancing, drinking and eating. He leans over to tell his good-looking (also available) friend a joke about you and everything that you lack. They burst into laughter. You know it's true, you know it is. He doesn't like you either. Bastard.

Noise.

Revoked Membership

I was just a lean boy of thirteen when I was kicked out of the "boy's" club. Was told to take my things and go home because I wasn't interested in playing sports, fighting, or chasing girls up and down the block. With time, I got over it. Had to. What it boiled down to was less time fighting over some nonsense and more time to perfect my cover of Gloria Gaynor's freedom anthem, "I Will Survive." That was 1979.

Later, as an undergraduate student, the "black" club snatched my membership card. I wasn't, nor was I ever, or will I ever be, "cool" black. More often, I am cast as "geeky" black, glazed with a little "radical" black thrown in for good measure. That was 1988.

Much later, I was booted out of the "gay" club. But that was fine with me, because I started that fight on purpose. That was 1995.

From the beginning, my only intention was to chill. To simply take a load off. To find a comfortable space with people I thought I shared a commonality with who would allow me the creative and breathing space to grow and mature. I craved a place in which I could be all I could be and more. I wanted to be a me that even I couldn't articulate and imagine, because I was still growing and being. I wanted to live.

When I was initiated into the "gay" club, I was beside myself with joy. I had the qualifications, the necessary experience, and a rather cute face. Rising through the ranks quickly, I encountered a few problems here and there, like internalized racism and heterophobia, but, for the most part, it was clear sailing. Then the penny dropped. Living would have to wait.

"He hangs around too many heterosexual women," said a former friend.

"He thinks he's better than us," retorted another.

"He uses too much profanity in his work," said a fellow struggling writer.

Guilty as charged. Except for the motherfuckin' remark about my use of too much goddamn profanity. I loathe cursing.

Anyway, after I was exposed for the individual I was and was about to be escorted out of the club, something inside me clicked. No, fuck that, I'm not going anywhere. This is my culture, my life, my world. I'll do what I damn well please. And I don't need a club, group, or any organization to tell me I matter. So there.

After years of reflection, the best thing that ever happened to me was that I was kicked out of these lousy clubs/organizations/institutions/jails, because I didn't either believe or fully understand what the owners believed anyway. I was just forming and wanted to be a part of something, to be loved and cherished. I signed on for love, not abuse. I wanted to live.

As a boy child, any effeminacy you might exhibit is generally snuffed out by your father, your uncles, your peers, or any other random man who feels it's his right to regulate your behavior. As you got your ass beat, the community watched and did nothing. And such was my community, which was largely black.

Being "black," or, rather, being accused of being "not black" has scared many of us into submission, to a standard of what's generally thought of as "stereotypical" black. You know what I'm talking about. In an attempt to be "down," you speak fluent "ebonics," wear your hair natural, talk loud about being black and proud (even though you probably don't believe it). Most importantly, you ridicule any brother or sister who doesn't fit this artificial standard of "blackness."

When we fully realize that that "light" skin color, fine hair texture, light eye color, being financially solvent, or speaking the King's English could never be better or worse than "dark" skin, full lips, wide hips, nappy hair, and living in the ghetto from check to check, then we might be able to look each other in the eye, indeed in the other's soul, and find love. Real love. Love that cannot be judged, cannot be found in the color of one's skin. Love that means we are people, and need not prove anything to anyone, ever! This, I think, is living.

Let me 'fess up. I think all black people are alright. I ain't gotta agree with them, live their lifestyles or be around them 24/7, but I recognize their right to be, and my right to love them. Nobody gets thrown away. Not even homos and lesbians.

Now, as for the "gay" club, it is probably the easiest club to quit due to all the bullshit I've put up with over the years. Even more than "straight" culture, gay culture is hermetically sealed. Physical appearance means everything resulting in an obsessive focus about the way you look. Will I be picked, will I be chosen? First of all, what is a "gay" life? Is it just a sexual preference or is it a culture? For me, sexuality can inform your life, but it's not a life. And now that mainstream media is trotting all these hysterically funny gay minstrels out on television and film, things are gonna get worse before they get better. Remember how long it took before black people were actually accepted as humans in this society? No? That's because it hasn't happened yet, chuckles. The mammies, coons and bucks are still dancing, but are now joined by a hysterically funny queer boy who knows all about makeovers.

Let me tell you, dating in the gay scene is a lot like shopping in a war zone. Bits of bodies litter the field of combat. An arm here or there, bodies barely breathing, part of a head with brains spilling out. Damn near everyone in some form or fashion has been hurt, discarded, or mistreated, and is trying very hard not to say it, not to fall apart in someone's arms, because we're all men, right? And men do not cry. But they do die, and sometimes we die and stay alive.

As you get older, things tend to get worse. You might simply resolve to give dating up. Everyone appears to be looking for something young and pretty, preferably with money, which is cool, but like everything in this world, things change.

Bar any unforeseen circumstances, we all get older, our bodies lose their youthful appearance, lose their vitality. Many young brothers are hunted, used, and abused because of what they represent–time passed, a time perhaps squandered. Many of us brothers spend an inordinate amount of time in front of the mirror, fearing the day we too may–excuse me, will–become obsolete on the market.

We are walking wounded when we apply for membership. What needs to be recognized is that membership only means you are a member. It doesn't mean that your masculinity, your race or your sexual preference makes you better than anyone else. It simply means you have found some people who believe what you believe–or rather, what you *think* you believe. Once you start flexing your curiosity, intellect, or spirit in a manner seen as threatening to the group, you'll be served your walking papers.

CHAPTER TWO: Them

Attention Homophobes: Something to Be Scared About

Brothers: When I write for a publication, I usually write for homie-sexuals like myself. But this particular essay was written for the average self-identified heterosexual man or woman. If you wouldn't mind, copy it and give it to some heterosexual; leave it on the train, make copies, tack it lamp posts, under windshield wipers. Whatever you have to do to get the word out.

You'll never guess what happened to me the other day. I was sitting on the train, and this good-looking brother got on and sat directly across from me. He was staring at me, and you know me, I looked back at him and shot him a smile. Then the damnedest thing happened. He folded his newspaper, rose out of his seat, bent down over me and asked me very softly if I was a faggot. I said, "why, yes I am," and added, "may I suck your big black dick?"

At that moment, the train's doors opened. The guy sort of backed away from me, out the door and onto the subway platform. I jumped up and followed him. He looked back, surprised to see me trailing him, at which point he began running. I dropped my bags and started running after him, and pretty soon we're running down the street, sideswiping passersby, dodging folk.

He darts down a side street and I'm hot on his trail. I tackle him, and he's screaming and hollering. I sucker punch him in the face and tell him to shut up, you know you want me. You've always wanted me. You been checking me out on the train for some time now. I know what you want. And I'm a give it to you right here.

So I put my knee on his neck and tell him not to move or I'll really get busy crazy on his ass. I unzip his pants (I unzip my pants) remove my knee and slap him in the face with my d....

We interrupt this essay for a very important announcement about bananas. We at Banana Central care about you and the bananas you purchased today, and we want to share a little information about those tasty little yellow friends of ours. Did you know that edible bananas originated in the Indo-Malaysian region reaching to northern Australia? We don't know about the ones that aren't edible. Anyway, today's modern edible banana is known by many names: bananier, nain, canbur, curro, and plantain, but you can just call it "banana!" Did you know bananas are the most popular fresh fruit in the United States? Well, they are! They have appeal, and they have "a peel" that comes off easily, they ripen after they've been picked, there is a generous supply all year, and, to top it off–they are cheap! Bananas have both a high amount of carbohydrates as well as potassium, which also makes them the fruit of choice for many athletes. To further ripen bananas, leave them on the table at room temperature for a couple of days. Once ripe, you can store in the refrigerator for 3 to 5 days. The peel may turn brown in the refrigerator, but the fruit will not change. Avoid bananas with brown spots that seem very soft. Avoid them like the plague. Select bananas with a nice color, specific for the variety. Choose fruit that is firm and free of bruises. Best eating quality has been reached when the solid yellow skin color is speckled with brown. Bananas with green tips or with practically no yellow color have not developed their full flavor. So be patient! Bananas are overripe when they have a strong odor and smell like liquor. Toss those bananas, and get your self some more! After all, they are cheap. To you and your family, from us and our families at Banana Central, good eating!

We now resume our scheduled essay, "Attention Homophobes," already in progress.

".....aaaaag, but I want some more," cried the man, "gimme some more, it's all I ever wanted, come on, pleeeeeeze!" But I would not be deterred. I told the man that I had made a terrible, terrible mistake and that I don't know what came over me. He certainly had the right to run away from me when I offered to blow him. "No, no, come on, man, give me that hot *bleepity bleepity bleep* one more time. Come on, put it on me....I gotta go home soon. Please...." I couldn't lie to myself. After I fed him my hot *bleepity bleepity bleep* I immediately felt bad. He lay there like a pancake that was turned over too quickly, soggy, undone–the pitiful bastard. I thought to myself: should I give this guy another swing on the Steven Express, or should I take my bad behavior home and repent for hunting down yet another heterosexually-acting/identified guy? I had to make up my mind quickly as I was getting a woody thinking about tagging this brother's nicetightpuckering a....

We interrupt this essay for one more important message about bananas:

For those of you who just tuned in, we at Banana Central want to make sure that you take care of your bananas. Caring for this fruit is easy–just remember these tips. If the banana is green, let it be! If it's yellow, it's mellow. But for really great taste, wait until your banana gets those brown spots that look like the ones on your uncle's face, and then it's ready to eat! To you and your family, from us and our families, we wish you the best at Banana Central.

We now resume our scheduled essay, "Attention Homophobes," already in progress.

..........sssss. oh yeah.....oh...ummmm....dayum.....

Dicksuckers Anonymous

Walk with me for a moment through a few scant paragraphs about curing homosexuality. The time you spend here will yield not only valuable information, but also a passel of giggles.

I have been a manhandler most of my adult life and have had an awful lot of experiences with the male species. A good chunk of time has been spent with men who were less than convinced that they were totally–ah, how would I say it?–weekend lollipop lickers. As opposed to career dicks, like yours truly. These men are convinced that, with just a little desire and a dram of God, they can kick their weekend proclivities in snap, that their natural feelings for men can be "fixed," that they can, with the love of a good, strong, fertile, woman, kick this dirty little habit for good.

It doesn't work. It never works. It can never work. To all weekend lollipop lickers: You can't stop wanting that physical connection–you just leave it alone for awhile. You only bide your time by hanging out with women. At most, you can become bisexual. Below are three short scenarios from men who have tried to become heterosexual because, well, it's easier to do and pays better socially.

Man number one: this guy was married and had a man on the side. When I met him I was as dumb as they come. I thought I could save him from a life of heterosexuality. My love would save all of us. The only thing I ended up saving was my own hide, and barely. Man number one's parents (his father was a preacher) sent him to a therapist in order to understand why their lovely son loved other people's sons. They tried throwing holy water on him and berating him every chance they had. He became an upstanding citizen in the community, in his father's church. The gay clung to him like a donut in a cop's mouth. He's still married and still sharing his sausage with other men. Needless to say it didn't take.

Man number two: he was just this side of twenty, a

Southerner who had moved to the big city to make his fortune as an actor. We met, and soon after, we were lovers. He had been raped ("encouraged" to fuck a man in front of a "producer" who gave him a "man" as a present) and was always preoccupied with what gay life meant, at least to him. We couldn't hold hands walking in Harlem. We couldn't kiss in public. We couldn't *be*. And after he came back from a trip to his parent's home for the holidays, he broke up with me. Said he wasn't going to be gay anymore. Gay was bad. He hoped to get married one day. His religion said homosexuality is a sin. Basically, what he said to me was, "Uh, Steven, I was talking to God and everything, and did you know that dicks aren't supposed to go into assholes?" Jeez. In this instance, God was the other man. Oh, and by the way, he's still gay today.

Man number three: he can only have sex with men who hurt him. He claims that this man thing is just a phase. He tells me this every time we talk. 'Nuff said.

Let me be clear: if a man doesn't want to have sex with another man anymore, then, well, okay, fine. But one cannot recover from homosexuality; that's just plain stupidity. That's like recovering from being black, and, although Clarence Thomas has tried hard to do just that, you can see it doesn't work. You can't seek asylum from desire. You can only divert your attention long enough to fool yourself (and no one else) that it's a phase, an inclination, an interest, but if you've thought about it, did it more than two times, have fantasies about foot longs, then show up early for practice, baby, because you are definitely on the team.

Eye for Eye

I've always said that if I wanted to date regularly, I'd take my happy ass to church. After all, we lesbians, homosexuals, gays, butt busters, carpet lickers, or whatever you want to call us, have been leading choirs, scrubbing down pews, and ironing the pastor's robes for millennia. What you probably don't know is that we've been secretly planning a mutiny of sorts. Right about now, we've got just about all of our men in place–choir directors, deacons, in addition to all those single guys that everybody's always trying to fix up–all in position to take over the church, and after that, the entire world! Hahahahahahahahahahaha!

We've been learning hymns in order to replace all the straight women in the church with "hims." At least those with no fashion taste. We've poisoned the holy water. Missing bibles–we took them. Short on the collection plate? We took it. Who do you think stole your car while you sat in church praying? That would be us. When praying, we poofs whisper silently to God for the complete and utter destruction of all heterosexual people everywhere. We figure the least we can do is return the love you've shown us for years.

Our goal? We fairies want full rights as citizens, just like anybody else. We want to walk hand-in-hand in public without being taunted or eventually run down like dogs by an angry, sanctimonious mob. We want to make love in peace, and that means without the slightest thought to our safety. We are tired of people worrying their little hearts out about what we do in bed. We would like to see what life would be like without being scared. We want our love of self back. And we plan to take it.

But let me be candid. I confess: you rabid heteros were right. We bulldaggers and sissies want everything you think and more. We want your wives and sisters, husbands and brothers. After all, they have made it more than clear that they want us. We men want to be able to wear dresses, flouncy ones, kinda like the ones they have in Scotland, but with full accessories. Our sister contingent wants full access to every tit bar in the state of the union, short hair cuts, and yes, boots. Together we would like more shoe stores and better dance clubs and bars with bathrooms clean of graffiti that says, "you's nigga lesbos need to fuc off!

Silly stuff, right? Ah, I don't think so. We homie-sexuals want to have as much fun as possible. Makeup for the boys? As much as we can smear on our hairy-ass faces. The buzziest of buzz haircuts for my lezzies-in-khakis. I personally want a man burning in the kitchen, one hard at work, and one writhing on the bed, so that I can eat the best foods, travel the world and buy what I want at a moment's whim, and have fresh booty at my literal disposal. In short, daddy wants it all! Okay, so the revolution hasn't really started yet, but I'm waiting on it. Mark my words, the sissies will prevail!

Since church is our preferred site for taking over the world, allow me to read from a few pages of my own complicated experience. As a wee young lad with cheek of peach, I'd disdainfully toddle off to church with my mother and siblings. My sweet mother, bless her pious heart, would yank me along and purposely sit between me and my brother. If I had had my way I'd perpetually knock him upside the head with a Bible out of sheer boredom. We attended a Lutheran church, and all I know about Lutheranism is that Lutherans have a very unexciting church by Baptist standards. No choir belting out any soul-stirring hymns. Our rotund ladies sat quiet and demure instead of wrestling on their backs in the aisles with the Holy Ghost. Staying awake at church was a full-time job, one where it was hard to keep a straight face. This here was one snore of a God, a Son and a Holy Ghost.

Although I never heard any homophobic remarks spewing from our white pastor's mouth, that doesn't mean anything because, well, I wasn't listening anyway. It was only in my late teens that I felt I needed some religion, because I was feeling the heat (puberty) and didn't want to feel the heat (hell).

Boy, did I try to be a good Christian. I read the Bible religiously (not the whole thing, just exciting books like Job and Revelations over and over). I practiced being Christ-like. I treated others like I wanted to be treated. I generally left them alone. I forgave and never forgot. I hung myself up on a cross before anyone got to me (thanks, homophobia.) I wore crucifixes and everything. I wanted to believe in the Bible, I did. In fact, I was panting for "Revelations" to get a-going. All that Armageddon stuff had me slobbering for the end to come like yesterday.

I always had mixed feelings about Christianity. After taking a black history course in college, my suspicions were confirmed: this here was a WHITE PEOPLE's religion. History illustrates just how Europeans used this religion to justify all kinds of madness, particularly the Transatlantic Slave Trade. Popular belief among slave masters in those parts was that if you served your earthly master, you could go on to serve your heavenly master. Whathefuck? *More masters?* You've got to be kidding me. These philosophies were further buttressed by my community—sinful, sanctimonious creatures who were constantly invoking the name of God to reject, judge, and abuse others, altogether behaving abominably. I lost what little bit of faith I had mustered and gained a profound loneliness. In this gray space, I began speculating on the existence of a God in the way it had been taught to me. The end result of my varied experiences, good and bad, but mostly rotten, was that I walked away thinking Christianity is a beautiful religion (I mean, it's not Satanism, right?) polluted by far too many wackos who can't handle their own business for sticking their noses in yours. But I digress.

Many a moon I sat with many thoughts about Christianity which did not feel right to me. The whole notion of being saved failed to move and impress. All I saw was Jesus being used as a perpetual coupon: redeemable as soon you fuck up. *Oh Lord Jesus, save my rotten ass soul!* This seemed like soul insurance purchased from a snake oil salesman. I can only imagine how much more tedious and horrible a few of the "saved" people I know would be if they weren't able to invoke Jesus's name at will. There would be no buffer, no spiritual whipping boy to take the heat for some dregs' reprehensible behavior.

Everywhere I go, people tell me I have to know the Lord, know the Lord, know the Lord. Does the Lord know *me?* Or even care to know *me?* Simply put, I respect Christianity, but my spirit doesn't speak this particular language. And I don't fully get the role of a minister. To be frank, I don't believe God needs an intermediary, an agent, a spin doctor, or an image consultant. If you're Everything, then you don't need anything. Everything is already inside; to me it's all about accessing it. Everything is God, good, bad, or indifferent. I've learned that if I really want to see what your "God" is all about, all I need to do is look at you and see, hmmm, what has He done for you lately?

I've always felt that any religion that relies solely upon coercion tactics to get more sheep into their flock–like pushing images of a devil poking your ass with a trident for eternity–is doomed from the start. It befuddles me. As if numbers were the final arbiter in the "what's right and true" contest. "The-more-us-the-more-we're-right" mentality. I don't care how many people believe in God; it don't mean I got to. But let me add this: the practicing Christians who I know and love aren't scheming to convert me in a tearful, lonely moment; they're too busy living a life of truth, leading by example, taking care of themselves, and being loving and compassionate to other people. You know, being Christ-like.

So be warned: if you see me in church, don't be fooled; I am on a mission: cruising or simply aiding my comrades in the quest to take over all churches everywhere. First the church and then the world! Peeking out from behind a hymn book, I will scout the scene for brethren who covertly hide their shotguns and knives in their suit coats. Let's see how God likes that.

We shall overcome.

A Few Lines for Homo Haters

Joe Public knows next to nothing about homosexuality. Oh, he may have sucked a dick or two, but he was young and that was his cousin; it was nothing. He knows less of it than I do of why people get married and then end up hating the other person for ruining their lives. Still, he behaves and thinks in a manner that fascinates me to no end. He (and I am speaking specifically to men, even though there's evidence that many women are just as kooky) desperately wants to believe three things about homosexuals: that homosexuality is a choice, that it is a sickness, and that the perpetrators are recognizable. Believing all of this crap, he thinks, would make his life so much easier, mainly because if he wanted to indulge in a little male-to-male play, then his chances of being suspected, much less caught, would be slim.

Let's take a minute to squash all the dumb things men think about men who have sex with other men. This is easy.

1) <u>Homosexuality is a choice.</u> Yeah, and so is ignorance. Folks choose to act on their feelings, which are as natural as breathing. I don't care how many studies are conducted that explain how some poor slob's X and Y chromosomes got mixed up because his mother was eating broccoli 8 months out of her pregnancy, how many people claim to be cured of this "disease" (they were just tasting goods), or how many people believe that dicks belong in vaginas and not assholes. I am not moved. Here's a clue: Don't like it, don't do it.

2) <u>Homos are sick.</u> Sick? Yeah, sick of everybody trying to determine the course of their lives. Like, back the fuck up, okay? It would make you sick, too, if you were constantly being bombarded with vitriolic rant from mom and dad and any random passerby. Yeah, that would make you sick, too. Here's another clue: mind your own business.

3) <u>Homos are easy to spot.</u> Sure we are. Hahahahahahahahahahahahahahahahahahahahahahahahahahahahahahah

ahahahahahahahahahahahahahahahahahahahahahahahah
ahahahahahahahahahahahahahahahahahahahahahahahah
ahahaha. Ha.

Let's be clear about one simple fact: people who are
homophobic are just ugly. Ugly like curled up toes on bent up
feet topped off with yellowed toenails. Stay away from them.
They will contaminate your mind. They are not fun to have at
parties.

Homophobes: if you don't like homosexuality, fine. Don't
be one, and do us a favor, and leave the rest of us the hell alone.

The Low Down on the Down Low

Gay is not synonymous with HIV/AIDS, just as black male is not synonymous with criminal. But when one examines the spate of media attention paid to this phenomenon called DL (for "down low," a culture consisting of men who have sex with other men but do not consider themselves gay), one sees that not only is black gay culture viewed as criminal, but it is also presumed guilty of harboring an unidentified silent killer in heterosexual clothing.

When the Centers for Disease Control recently released a study stating that 30% of gay black men (or black gay men) are infected with the HIV virus, the popular media went berserk. Ironically, the public was treated to tales that weren't so much about black gay life, but about the fears of the larger white and black communities about the AIDS pandemic. Print, broadcast and cyber media delivered potent cocktails of stories that mixed homophobia, Hip-Hop, and HIV/AIDS. Panel discussions were held. Black gay leaders and activists were summoned for sound bites concerning DL culture, and more than a few of those men expressed their frustration and anger at those "trifling, down-low, confused, and dangerous DL men."

But let's put it all in context.

In 1995, I came out to my father. He was the only person other than my mother whose opinion mattered to me. I told him the "news" over the phone. He listened quietly. After the initial shock, he was surprisingly supportive. Then it was my turn to listen. He told me that he was worried that I could be marginalized, that I could get fired or hurt, and that I should keep my business to myself—on the down low. My father was also fond of saying that a man shouldn't do in the dark what he's ashamed to do in the light. I live somewhere in between his two comments, comfortably.

That said, I am a man who celebrates a life that is sexually and intimately involved with other men. I occasionally publish stories about my experiences, exploring my perceptions and feelings about race, culture, education, and, of course, sexuality. In effect, I am an "out" gay male, at least in print.

But let me also make it clear that if I were living life on the DL, that if I were not open about my homosexuality, it wouldn't be any of your business. Here's why:

Nearly every story I have read or seen or heard about DL culture talks about how dishonest these men are. That they are a danger to the community. That these insidious men should come out to their community and be their true selves. "Come out, come out, wherever you are," people say. "We will accept you as you are. Just tell us the truth."

Well, black people, y'all can't handle the truth.

I am personally confronted with all kinds of homophobia day in and day out, which, at times, I have to ignore in order to remain sane. Homo hate is everywhere: at the office, on the train, on the street, in my building, in stores, at church, on television, in books, films, and music. Damn near everywhere I look I see people talking about faggots, or I overhear some mother in the park telling her young male child, "don't be a punk, be a man," even though he is only a boy. Teenagers call each other fag to bolster their own fragile masculinities. Men jokingly call each other faggots. Sisters don't want no sissies around them. Parents disown their progeny.

Parentless, homeless, bamboozled, beat down, depressed, dispossessed.

Now, doesn't this sound great? Just a perfect, healthy, and wonderfully supportive environment in which brothers can reveal themselves. Yes, I think I shall encourage all the closeted men that I know to come out, be free, wave a Rainbow flag and kiss their boyfriends in public. If they don't, you can rely on me to admonish them for not being honest! Yes, I shall tell them that they have no right to their privacy, because the world says that they are being dishonest and that they need to reveal themselves for the good of the community. Forget being misunderstood, or being bombarded with all kinds of ignorance and injustices! Dem straight folks wanna know yo bizness!

Yeah, I'll get right on it.

I would be remiss if I didn't take a minute to talk about the black community's longstanding ambiguity concerning their menfolk and adulterous behaviors. For centuries, many men have led double lives, one as a faithful husband, and the other as an unconfined, free-wheeling bachelor. Before it even had a name, black folks condoned DL culture. Why else would it be a recurring theme in so many blues and jazz songs, with their messages of double lives, secrets, and acclaimed freedom? "Just don't let me find out about her," "T'aint nobody's business if I do," and so on. I've heard women, and a few men, deliver soliloquies about this idea all my life. All any man had to worry about was being circumspect.

So let's take this opportunity to set the record straight (haha). If a man is on the DL, that's his business. If he spends his time out having unprotected sex with men (or women), contracting venereal diseases and bringing them home to his girlfriend or wife or male lover, then that's another story. That's an issue of honesty, not sexuality—or, to the point, homosexuality. Honesty to the people we're involved with, especially the people we're sleeping with, is bottom-line crucial. But honesty to the whole damn world, especially a world prepared to hurt us for our orientation, is up to the individual.

The best thing that I can say about DL culture is that it may be just the kick in the pants that's necessary to keep healthy the very public conversation we seem to be having about black sexuality. And boy do we need to talk about it, for health's sake. Frankly, we don't have a choice. Whether you are gay, heterosexual, bisexual, or on the DL, you do not want to be left out of this conversation. As the early AIDS activists said, "Silence equals death."

If we can't talk to each other across perceived sexual boundaries, the walls of ignorance will just get higher. Black men and women will continue to put themselves at risk for catching HIV. Ignorance about one's sexuality will continue to be passed down from generation to generation. And perhaps, worst of all, after the dust has cleared, nobody will be left to talk about anything.

Open Letter to my Hetero Sisters

Oh boy, do I have a lot to say to you, and I hope you can hear it. For the longest time I have had to endure your worlds–how you feel about this dress or that bitch at work, but most frequently about the men in or not in your life. About how these men are married, incarcerated, or gay. So I thought I'd spend a few sentences about what the last comments look, smell and sound like to me. Fasten your seatbelts.

First of all, let's address the notion of the phantom black male–you know, the brother you feel you are *entitled* to, the one who is married, incarcerated or gay. On the one hand, I am so for you getting yours. I, too, want to see heterosexual couplings that are happy and healthy between people who are able to not only love each other unconditionally, but who will continue the propagation of the species, so get busy and make those babies, stat! But, sister, be clear that if a man loves other men, he was never an option for you. So stop running your mouth, acting as if Homo Tyrone betrayed you because he likes a little sausage in the morning, and at night. In this case it ain't all about you, and never was. You're just mad because he's cute and you are alone, period. I'll address this issue again a little later on.

Second, let me prick (sorry) the ballooned myth that all heterosexual sisters and homosexual brothers are a match made in heaven. Yeah, right. Not until we really communicate and be frank regarding the stereotypes about each other. There are some couplings, but overall we are at war. Face it: you might think I'm after your man. I might think your man is out fucking around on you, and jocking me, you know? Unfortunately, sometimes it's all true, and we both end up looking stupid because we were what? PLAYED!

So back to the "you just mad cuz you lonely" issue. I've got serious problems with some of you sisters because you want it easy. Too easy. Black woman meets black man and bam!, he's the

one and you'll get married, produce kids and both live happily
ever after, the end. If he's not the one, or happens to love other
men, then he's damaged goods. Wrong. Sour grapes, baby. You
only think like this because we (men who prefer other men)
ain't giving you none, and do not support this wack fantasy of a
"good" black man. Consequently, we're tossed into a pile of
"worthless" brothers. You know the ones I'm talking about. If
I've heard it once, I've heard it a skillion times: "If he ain't in jail,
he's married, got a girlfriend, got a white girl, or he's gay." Being
gay isn't an affront to my heterosexual sisters, but many of you
like to think so. That's your ego talking. Like anyone chooses
to be gay so they don't have to be with a sister. Furthermore if
a man is straight, he still has the option of choosing *another*
sister. Still, many sisters froth at the mouth when they peep a
brother who "looks" heterosexual, but is in fact gay. "He's fine,"
they'll say, but upon finding out he's not sexually available, "too
bad he's gay." Yeah too bad for you, but not me.

Third, I think it's important to offer this apology in writing
for the transgressions against black women that I have
committed. Even as I love you, I know I have been self-
centered, to say the least. Sometimes I'd only sought your
shoulder to cry on when I didn't have a date. When there wasn't
a man in sight, sure, we could hang out, cry, complain, and rant
about the lack of romantic love in our lives. But when I had a
man I wanted you to conveniently disappear. In those moments
I have been less than sympathetic to your needs. You'd turn up
the noise with your trials and tribulations with black men, and I
sat seething, thinking, "well, at least the world doesn't hate you.
You can kiss your man in public, damn near fuck him. Not me. I
have to hide because some asshole may decide that my life is
expendable and not one person, male or female, would come to
my rescue. Stick that in your cap." As you see, I was not above
dumping my oppression on you. Now I feel very different. I
apologize for my stupidity, pettiness, and lack of respect,
because now I realize that if I don't treat you better, how can I
ask you to do that for me?

I've witnessed (and combated) the rabid sexism among my brothers who on one hand describe women as "fish," and in the next breath greet another brother with a hardy "girrrrrrrrrrirl!" But like I said, the chasm runs deep because of stereotypes. We can't view each other as competition, because we're not. Are "good" black men at such a premium in this culture that we're willing to slit each other's throats for a little love or dick? Frankly, all the hype about not being able to find a good black man may lie less in what black men are doing, but in our ideas about what constitutes one, you know? I'm not talking about settling for a brother who's trifling, self-centered, or ignorant of his past, cruel or indifferent to your needs. I'm talking about a revisioning of what your fantasies, I mean, standards are. I think a good man is... We've all got to fill in this blank for ourselves. If anyone thinks that this is an easy exercise, it ain't. What you want out of a man should tell you all about yourself. If you don't like what you see, well, maybe it's time to change.

My best of friend of 13 years is heterosexual, and she and I both struggled to move past the stereotypes about one another to build a strong alliance that serves to uplift us both. Hard work, yes, but well worth the effort. We could cut through the bullshit and tell each other the deal about our romantic interests. We are not unique. There are plenty of sisters and brothers exactly like us. But I wouldn't hold my breath waiting for other sisters and brothers to fall in line, because, like I said, building bridges is hard work.

However, I cannot apologize for the behaviors of my brothers; that's on them. I hope you will continue to reach out—some of us are waiting. Please don't be deterred, distracted, or disheartened by the stereotypes lumped on women by gay men in general, or the attitudes of some truly ignorant brothers. They don't know about how wonderful you really are. Maybe they're afraid of your undeniable beauty. We are not all out to get all the "straight" brothers. You can't get what ain't coming to you, or take what ain't yours. And for the brothers reading this, check yourself and delete from your vocabulary the word "fish" and other derogatory words that you commonly use to describe sisters. Think about how you might take a sister's hand. We are all trying to love. Be courageous and look in the mirror. Let's put an end to all this madness.

Why We Don't Cry

Okay, sisters, you say you want sensitive men. You say you want men who are able to cry, tell you their secrets, and share their innermost thoughts. You want men to be open.

Puh-lease. You don't want no sensitive man. What you want is a man who can sit down and at any given time tell you how he feels. Sisters want a man who can communicate. But don't let him cry, oh no. That's not the kind of "sensitive" man you sisters want, right? Give me some room to break it down, okay?

Sensitivity is a highly subjective term, and many brothers feel it's akin to being seen as less than a man. For many brothers (and sisters), sensitivity equals feeling, which equals weak. I don't think I ever met a woman who wanted a "weak" man. See the problem? No, you need some more.

Black men walk the wobbling tightrope that is American masculinity daily. Fraught with all kinds of danger, he carefully chooses when, where, and how he will reveal himself. Any of us brothers could slip and fall and boom!, hit the pavement face down because there is no safety net. Because everybody and everybody's momma believes a man should be a man, but, they haven't the slightest clue as to how that's achieved in this sexist, racist, and homophobic culture.

Dig, many a brother feels that if he's caught doing something that's not manly (like crying in front of a woman) then he won't get his. The fear is that his homies won't respect him, and that the sisters will ignore him. Who will love him? Nobody. So, of course, he chooses to be silent, to generally not express his feelings except maybe with his fists. To let all his anger, rage, and frustration fester, and, eventually explode. This calls to mind a scene from *The Salt Eaters*, by the late great Toni Cade Bambara. The author described the feelings of a troubled young black man while he was raping a 46-year-old woman: "Be good to me, bitch, cause no one has so you take the weight."

Well, now. With that said, let me tell you all what type of "sensitive" man you *really* want.

You want a sensitive man who will share his feelings in a way that's comfortable for you. Check this. True stories.

Billy had been going out with Anna for a while. They were college sweethearts. Something happened one day to Billy, and while he and Anna talked, he teared up, but did *not cry*, in front of Anna. Billy told me, "After that, Anna changed. She stopped calling me as much; whenever we got together, she seemed uncomfortable around me."

Sisters, remember that Billy didn't even cry. So let's move on to the poor sap who dared to show his "feelings" to a woman who, like plenty of women I know, claim they want sensitive men.

My good friend Alicia told me one day about this guy she was dating named Tom. She and Tom were having problems, and Alicia, thinking the end was near, decided to break it off.

"He broke down in front of me," Alicia recalled, staring into the distance for a second. Then she broke out into a fierce, uproarious laughter. "It turned me off! He was crying hard, too! It was ugly!"

It was a brother's ultimate nightmare sprung forth from the bowels of hell! She apparently lost all respect for him because he came apart in front of her. This got me heated. He was sensitive, and what did he get? Dogged out. Brother thought he could tell his woman all about his heartache. Apparently not.

My best friend Carla, when I told her about this essay, leaned over and told me that when her ex-boyfriend shed tears when they were in the middle of a break-up, she was overjoyed. "Some man crying for me? Oh, yeah, I like that!"

Here's the scorecard thus far: if he sniffs or tears up, sisters are liable to get leery and frown. If the crocodile tears start a-dropping, then sisters are bound to freak out and run out the door. But if he's crying for you and *you like it,* because it makes you feel good, then alright, cry on, brother. Hmmm.

My thing is this: do sisters *really* want a sensitive man, and if so, why? For partners, friends? Ridicule? I've read plenty of books and articles by black women, watched television and films, and the *Lifetime* network (yeah, like there are a bunch of black women on that channel). I'm privileged to have had numerous conversations with many sisters I know and love and the question remains in my head, do you really want sensitive brothers? And just how "sensitive" should they be?

Let me say this upfront. Many brothers have a hard time expressing their feelings, and plenty can't express a diversity of emotion, period. So I can understand a sister's reaction (surprise?) to a brother choking up, gurgling, boo-hooing and the like, but still. Brothers got it hard on that tip. Which leads me to a little story I think is appropriate here.

Octavia tells me of a friend of hers, a single mother who admonishes her little boy not to cry, because, you know, he's a boy child. However, she has no problem crying in front of him. That's messed up. I know what's up with this behavior. Some stupid belief that if you don't rough up a boy when he's younger, then others will take advantage of him. Let me say for the record that a man who's in touch with his feelings is a strong man, which is what sisters claim they want, right?

I have experienced and witnessed boys being "roughed up" all of my life, by mothers, fathers, other relatives, and even strangers. Can you imagine how painful it is to be told you can't cry when it hurts? The realization of the pain coming? *The very thought of the reaction* of damn near everyone in the community forbidding you to cry. It hurts more. It deadens. It happened to me and it paralyzed me for years. I never forgot what it was like to hear the phrase "boys don't cry." Over and over and over, like a mantra. And it was a stanking-assed lie. Of course, we little boys cried, but you all didn't want to see the tears. Now, there ain't no tears and you say you want "sensitive" men. Puh-lease.

By my calculation, sisters, you've either dated, married, or loved one or more of us damaged brothers. How fun was that? And you all know that many of us have this problem, so why jet when it gets a little tough? Is this what we'll get when we try to give you a little of what's brewing, churning, and burning inside of us? Please, please, please, give us a little love and understanding; don't scrunch up your nose. Don't go running out the door when we need you to be strong, because, really, we need you to be strong for us, *with* us. Yeah, I know that many of you have shed enough tears to fill every pond, stream, lake, sea, and ocean, and now you're fed up. All I can say is that it's gonna take some patience on both sides to get us through this mess.

I also suspect what's lurking behind all this "I want a brother who's in touch with his feelings" business is a high strain of homophobia. He can't be too in touch with his feelings, right, sisters? If he is, you might think he wants to model your underwear on the Jerry Springer Show. So do men have to be gay to be in touch with their feelings? To cry, to show emotion, to let you know that we (and we know that you know) hurt too? Gay brothers get all the breaks when it comes to being *seen* as sensitive brothers. Maybe that's because there's no imminent danger of swapping booty with him, you think? And on top of that, it's a big lie. Some of my gay brothers can be just as unexpressive, sexist, and damaged as their heterosexual counterparts.

So, now that you know that we know that you know, give us a break. We'll try to do better. Let us cry. That way, we can all do better.

CHAPTER THREE: ME

The Death of Steven, Inc.

Heru (my best friend and business partner) called me recently to tell me that my website doesn't represent me. That my quirky insights into life, love and the pursuit of poonanny, are largely absent from my site. That I am throwing up filler on my BLOG (web log) section without a context. Get this. He says that people who know me know that I have a take on life that is honest and doesn't take itself too seriously. That he and others—meaning my friends, countless admirers and Stevenites—should want to tune in everyday to my website to find out what shit I've conjured up in words. That I need to exploit my Steven adventures more. Talk more about my fine-assed self.

I was like, *jigga what?*

Let me offer some background here and then you'll better understand what it's my pretty little dented head. Years ago when Heru and I ran One Step Further, a sexual education and advocacy company that serviced black and Latino men (and did we!) who are intimately and sexually involved with other men, I jokingly started up a "company" called Steven, Inc., to describe my work outside of my work with OSF and at the library.

So, anyway, whenever I was busy with a project and couldn't talk I'd say that I was doing Steven, Inc. stuff. Or when I wanted to get out of a commitment, or didn't want to be bothered, I'd say I had some Steven, Inc. business to attend to. Steven, Inc., freelance writing, facilitating workshops, panel presentations, massage classes, the Black Gay and Lesbian Archive, and whatever else I wanted to do.

Hahahahahahahahahahaha. Ha. Hahahahahahahahahahahahahahahahahhahahahahahahahhahahahahahah ahahahaha.

I was a fucking monster.

Steven Inc. was a good idea at the time (2000-2002), but

then I got bored with it because, well, I got a whiff of my own farts and I got on my OWN damn nerves. I was freelancing like a madman, always on the make for a new gig, always publishing something or other, mainly reviews–which if I may be so bold to say were frequently useless, at least to me. What I learned after penning nearly two hundred of them is that good criticism isn't about if a CD/book/film is good or bad; it should seek to inform the reader, place the art in various contexts, and interpret (and never assume) what the artist was trying to do. I was okay at it. Frankly I could write an okay review in my sleep. Real criticism takes patience and care, neither of which I fully possessed.

In addition to writing reviews, ed-op pieces and personal essays, there was the archive, the endless projects, the speaking engagements, the parties, the openings, the trips to California, London and Japan...oh it was just bloody awful. Ran myself down to the ground and ended up ill as result. So, I quit freelancing full-time and decided to concentrate on smaller projects that would not stress me out day to day where I could focus and still get a good night sleep. I started doing yoga and immediately felt better. Ahhh.

Then 2003 came and the urge returned. Steven, Inc. reared its ugly yellow head. FEED ME! FEED ME! You know how hard it is to turn down writing gigs? It's like my dick in the morning–HARD. Had to turn down three writing gigs because I was knee-deep in co-editing a small book Think Again. Among other writing gigs, I had also penned a bio on John F. Matheus, a Harlem Renaissance writer and foreign language professor for a Harlem Renaissance encyclopedia. That was work.

Some context might be useful here. I wanted to be famous when I was a kid. I wanted to do something important for others. I wanted folks to recognize me on the street and love me. Now that I have some self-esteem and I am accomplishing goals that I feel are important (writing, the Black Gay and Lesbian Archive, *art in harlem*, a celebration of art and performance in New York City) I am not overly concerned with being famous and, in many cases, recognized or, in some cases, even liked.

In fact, I know that I wouldn't be any good at being famous. I am not camera ready under any circumstances (I tried practicing my smile in the mirror, and it looks like some kicked me in the nuts.) I cannot be "on" all the time. I am not cute. I don't have the energy or interest in pursuing cute as a full-time job, which, by my estimation, would entail far too many haircuts, trendy clothes, a shiny face, and eyebrow-pluckings. I am not invested in saying the right thing, and I know even less about what is right. You know who I am? I'm the guy who looks like he just got out of bed, eyes squinting, perpetually scratching his belly going, "what?"

And let's face it, I can be moody. Mad moody. I screen all calls all the time. Why? It might be *you!* You can count on me to walk past you on the street without saying hi if you don't see me first. Why? Maybe I don't wanna be bothered with you and your etiquette, dumb-ass. Ever think of that, chuckles? "Hi, how are you, how's the family, how's your writing coming along, did you hear that new CD by so-and-so that everybody bought so that must mean it's good, blah, blah, and more blah."

So anyway, the fame thing. This is what I have learned about fame. Being famous means being beholden to an idea or theory or status or group or gang or religion or perspective or way of being in the world. That's not me. I don't want to do anything to be respected, admired or whatever. Too much work, so little pay. If you like me, fine; if not, as my English teacher once told me: If you don't want me, I don't want you twice!

So I eschew the common scene in order to maintain my admittedly perverse perspective on life, and mainly my smart-assed mouth. I don't attend parties or gigs where people like me (intelligent, sexy, crazy, certified) are supposedly supposed to be. Who can be bothered with showing up at the same damn place, over and over, being a barnacle on the pop scene? I only have one outfit. Besides, I treasure peace of mind, a valuable thing in a city like New York where there's too much of everything, all at one time, in your lousy face generally when you don't feel like seeing, hearing, or smelling it.

But the one thing that Heru said that struck me as being useful in pursuing as a valid: I have a responsibly to make my website (indeed, my art) entertaining, engaging, and promoting the image I want out there. That my website is a property of the marketing and public relations division of all that I wish to accomplish while I am still here, living the life of a fake-ass player.

Okay, so this is how I am going to do it:

Whenever I feel like trotting out any little story about my life, what I ate or wore or felt like doing on any given Tuesday morning, I will. Or what I did, who I did, and why I did 'em, I might just tell you. And perhaps most interesting to you, what I think about you, you insecure, pop culture slut who wants everyone to like you and so you've spent your life being whoever it is you think the world wants you to be.

Stay plugged.

Dicks Don't Kill People...

Okay, so you can die from AIDS-related complications. Big fucking deal. Statistics show that you can also die being mowed down by a beer-swilling drunk driver on your way to work, knifed in the back by a stinking derelict in the subway, develop a nifty cancer in your throat. Fall backwards down a flight of stairs and break every bone in your body. Get chopped up by a dejected lover. Stand in or below a collapsing building. Be pushed suddenly from a speeding car. Be electrocuted, drowned, or beaten to smithereens. We all die somehow, someway. This is the contract we all signed as we decided to incarnate–it's in the fine print. No offense, but these are the breaks that break up the body and file it down, down to dust.

These are just a few of the many faces of death. It's irrefutable that all of us are just a breath away from our last. The benefit of keeping this unavoidable fact in mind could serve as inspiration to live every day to the fullest, as if it were your last day. Or it could depress the hell out of you. But let's try to use this knowledge for the best. Come on, get out from under your bed and read on. Come on, please, I promise to go slowly.

If death is always a possibility, then you are free, right? You are free to do what you want with your life. That means get your sorry, sanctimonious, judgmental ass off the couch and try living your dream, no matter how ridiculous or unattainable it may seem. What escapes many of us is the fact that dreams, along with an occasional tasty hoagie sandwich, are all you have. When you consider the lesser choices: waste your time lying and cheating, committing slow suicide, or intentionally working to destroy another, living your dreams seems much more interesting and fun. And isn't that what life should be all about anyway, having fun, fun, fun? Sure it is!

Take me, your friendly neighborhood pipe-slinging scribe. I was one of those nervous, bone-thin scrappers who had the extreme good fortune to evolve into a fairly confident, if neurotic, man. A good deal of my time now is spent learning to be loving and compassionate. No fooling. I do not question my existence (I'm here to make folks laugh), worry about what racist white people are doing (I'm here to make them laugh), or try to look or act like Joe Average (but I will fuck him.) I work very hard at watching what I eat, and how I exercise, and praying and trying not to hurt people. All told, I am a relatively happy man who manages his crazy fairly well.

How did I get here? Abbreviated resume would look something like this. As a kid I wanted to be a pop singer. Day and night you could find me dancing and singing up a storm in my room, picking splinters out of my feet. I happily took up piano and voice lessons (exactly four lessons each), beat on my pillow with drumsticks until feathers flew (imitating Sheila E.), wrote lyrics to a shitload of wholly unsingable songs (which I often tried out on patient, if bemused friends and family members.) I brazenly entered talent shows with half-baked routines snatched from videos, ready to take home a prize only to ride home with a friend's arm around me: "hey, you were good, but maybe next time."

To support myself I sold vitamins, swept up hair in a barbershop, taught English and storytelling, waited tables, flipped burgers, tossed pizzas, mowed lawns, babysat children, delivered newspapers (for exactly one day), and hammered out term papers for others (yeah, ah, I know). Concurrently my spare time was used to improve my art, and working toward whatever else I wanted to do. Additionally I cut my teeth by freelancing for less than reputable newspapers and magazines to learn the craft and to collect clippings. I have given speeches, created art exhibitions, hosted talent shows and co-created a consulting company with a colleague. For every triumph, there were many more heart-breaking defeats. Yet each time I do something, I get better at it, and I am always interested in doing more for myself. Always. Ain't no stopping me, baby!

This blabbering should prove that there is no recipe or 10-step program to success, but I think it's important to put this in your head: in my own goofy and clumsy way, I try to live my dreams. Sure, there are war and poverty; sure violence spills out of the workplace, the home, and the streets where we live and make a living. Sure, people are dying of AIDS-related diseases, of cancer, of all kinds of ailments that have claimed many of our loved ones and friends. Sure, it hurts, sure it can be overwhelming, but in experiencing these rough hard-to-swallow, back-breaking, breath-snatching moments, I have gleaned one thing: to appreciate my weird little life view.

After seeing enough people die in film, on television, in real time, the thought occurred to me quite clearly that one day I could be mowed down by a beer-swilling drunk driver on my way to work. Or be knifed in the back by a stinking derelict in the subway. Or develop a nifty cancer in my tender throat. Fall down a flight of stairs and break every bone in my lithe body. Get chopped up by a dejected lover. Be pushed from a speeding car. Be standing in or below a collapsing building. Be electrocuted, drowned, or beaten to smithereens. Who knows when I'll be dancing my last jig all the way to the boneyard? I don't, do you? Tell me if you do. Let's have lunch sometime and we can plan my funeral.

Until the Grim Reaper shows up, this little piggy gonna go wee-wee-wee all the way to the drawing board, where I am designing my latest whatever. Writing dreams. World peace dreams. Fucktivities. You know what it's like to watch people whom you love and care about let their dreams die? They go limp but still live. To them, life is like a perpetual canker sore, an aching that never relents. What a disappointment. It's like finding out that all this time God didn't care about you and now you have to take up the slack. You either become ultra-judgmental or apathetic—or both—and are absolutely no fun at parties.

My only advice is to please, please, discover what you love and then live it. Try to remember that there are other people in the world who may need your help, so don't be a selfish jerk; help them out. Feed the hungry, clothe the naked, and give to the poor. Teach a class to a kid, visit a sick relative, or help clean up a community park. Find something that benefits the livelihood of others, because, face it, you may be helping make someone else's dream come true. The ratio of people who live their dreams vs. those who don't is staggeringly low. Share a little light with the world and you'll be surprised about how good it feels on your skin, your face, and your heart. Be connected to something other than your own little narcissistic self.

I have seen a lot of people that I care very deeply die, men and women who rarely, if ever, reached for what they wanted in life, and it set my little yellow ass on fire. I know people who claim that for some reason they aren't able to get this or that and I feel for them. I know what it feels like to be told you can't do something and to feel somehow that you were in some way gypped at birth. We all got our thing. Mine was being tagged a flaming sissy. How hard was *that* to overcome in an environment where everybody is bent on making you a "man," whether they know you or not? Like I couldn't be myself, I had to be this thing folks called a "boy," a regular "boy." I wanted to me be me. I tell you it was like breaking up concrete with your fingers.

But don't cry for me, Argentina, because, all told, this boy is all right. All my life I've been judged because I love men. Now that I regularly hang my hat in the homes of many other like-minded sisters and brothers, I am grateful for the lessons. I am compelled, no, driven to write the stories and tell the world about the ways we use oppression to beat each other about the heads: you know "you got more ___ so I hate you because it's easier than looking at myself" type of oppression. Living in fear and hatred stops the love process.

So, it is with sincerity that I say that dicks don't kill people, shame does. Shame from living a lie, shame from not sticking up for oneself, shame for feeling like a coward. Shame for believing all the lies that _____ told you when they said that you were a worthless piece of shit. Shame has killed enough of us and will continue to decimate brothers and sisters until we start loving ourselves despite what we look like, possess, or think we should be doing. Is it too simple to grasp? I think it is. I also think that if you can't imagine loving yourself, then you're in pathetic shape. I'm not talking about my-ass-looks-great-in-these-jeans love, or I-have-gobs of-cash-boy-I-feel-good love, I am talking about unconditional-even-when-you're-broke-alone-and-ugly kind of love. Ever felt that? Of course you haven't, you pop culture slut. Now, get off that damn couch and get living!

Again, dicks don't kill people; having no purpose in life is the killer. It blanches life and fleeces any healthy perspective out of the beauty and wonder of living. And, in short, it's no fun to be around anyone who is a sucker for suffering. Talk to anyone who is fearful of death, blames everyone for his/her troubles, and believes that life in general sucks–is probably not only a Republican, but also a jerk who lets his cereal go soggy as an excuse to weep. In short, a dick that actually kills people.

FrankenSteven

Some years ago, I had the opportunity to read my work on a panel featuring established and new black gay writers. Sitting to my left was E. Lynn Harris, and to my far right was James Earl Hardy. The room was full of supportive men and women, the day was beautiful, and I looked great! Everything was coming up Steven!

Yo, I was terrified! Felt like running under the stage. Had a constant urge to urinate. Prior to the program I was fine, confident, dry, secure. Had practiced my pieces, a few notes on the function of writing in my life, the role I see myself assuming as a black, brother lovin' artist.

Things didn't turn out as dandy as I planned. Frozen like a Popsicle, I wasn't in my body for more than three seconds of the more than two hours we, the writers, were given to present our material. Here's a sampling of what transpired:

I was the second writer to speak. After some tussling with the mike at my seat, I got up and went to the podium to read "Do Your Own Thinking," an essay. My voice cracked, sped up, slowed down, all on its own accord. I was so nervous, I couldn't really hear myself. I wondered what everyone–the other writers, the audience–thought. I was doing too much thinking!

After some polite applause, I read a poem called "So You Have A Gay Cousin." After I gave a little context about why I wrote the poem, feeling as if I botched up on it, I walked each word out slowly, hoping to minimize the cracking in my voice. I could hear my voice fade in and out; all the while I fought the desire to simply push the podium over and run out of the room. But I persevered, finished, and during polite applause, took my seat very, very unsatisfied with my performance.

Immediately I told myself, "Hey, it's my first time, I wasn't horrible." Then another self answered, "Wait a minute. I'm trying to hear the other writers." Then a third self launched in, "Can we read the essay again? I'm so sure I could do it better this time."

As I got myself together, E. Lynn leans over and says, "That was good." I think he said "very good," but I was too nervous to really hear anything at that point.

More dialogue from the inside:

"God, why in the hell am I here?"

"I wonder why James Earl is wearing an African outfit. I associate Africanness with being open, nice, and kind. He's a little defensive about his work. But at least he's got a book out. I like it. Lots of sex scenes in it and all."

While Hardy read a few passages from his erotic, butt-splitting, saliva-drenched, hole-gaping, cum-stained fiction, I made a mad dash out to pee. God, it felt good. Escape and release.

Yet more inside dialogue:

"E. Lynn is very humble. Makes me wanna finish Just As I Am. Okay, not really, but at least he's got a book out."

"I want to leave this place and never write another goddamned thing in my miserable little life."

"Oh, hush up and stop being so hard on yourself."

"I betcha that lil' James Earl can fight."

Then came time for Q and As, and I'm far too nervous to address any questions. I just pass the microphone back and forth to the other deserving, published writers. Oh, me.

"Why in the hell didn't you answer any questions?" yelled Alicia, then my publisher. "We've talked about all these things before, the writing process, the content, jeez. You just sat there, passing the microphone back and forth, back and forth. It was driving me crazy!" I dash out to pee for the second time and go back to Alicia, who is holding out one of my fliers. "Take this over to E. Lynn." I flatly refuse. She gets livid.

"Boy, you'd better get over there," she threatened. I'm frozen to my spot.

I can't think of a thing to say to E. Lynn or any of the other writers. Even during the Q and A, I decided that it was better to sit than to actively participate in the discourse. You would've thought I'd lost my mind. I always have something to say! I'm smart as all-get-out! I fucking amaze me!

It hit me after a few days. I shouldn't have been there on that stage mumbling like a 4th grader shuffling his feet. "FrankenSteven" should've burst through the doors and, in knocking me off the stage, would have grabbed the microphone and laid it on quick and thick.

"This is what I do. This is how I do it. Here it is. It gives you chills, don't it?"

"FrankenSteven" would've chosen the most passionate piece to read in order to squeeze a few tears out of the ready-to-cry. He would've dropped a few silences to emphasize the intensity of the work he was presenting. His eyes would've cast a spell over the room, making those in attendance pine for more of his work. Some would've left wondering where they could purchase the outfit he had on. Anything at all to remind themselves they had been touched, had been in his presence, had been present for the occasion of this marvelous gift.

Steven–that's me–needs space to write. He's not a celebrity, nor does he want to be one. He just wants to communicate through his work. Yet he knows he's got a pretty face and a good caboose to boot, pun unintended. He knows he has to haul it up and promote his work accordingly so. So, good work = appearances. Alicia said it's the only way to get the word out about the book, showing the fuck up. Being a public person means work. "FrankenSteven" must be constructed. I have the technology. I have the power. I have no choice. I'm in my laboratory now hooking up electrodes to my monster's head as we speak.

Voice. I have a tendency to speak fast. I dunno why, but I suspect it's because I think I know everything. Okay, I do know everything, but I could still manage to speak slower. Do....you...understand...the words...that are.......... You get what I am talking about. Calibrate my monster's voice to slooooow.

Pieces to Read. I have started asking my friends to look at my work, and preview a reading in front of them to see if it works. I'll bore the bejesus out of them first, before I drench some crowd with my rambling observations on life and loving the poonanny. "FrankenSteven" likes that. Bore, bore, bore them and then eat their brains.....arrrg!

Learn How to Act. This one is essential. Being "on" isn't one of my talents, but it's something I am learning to cultivate if I need it, like having a flashlight in a blackout. I commonly associate being "on" with being phony, but that's not necessarily true. You can be "on" and not be a phony, right, sugar plum? I want people to see, hear, and feel me. Move my limbs in a comfortable way. Touch a shoulder of a listener while I read. Suppress urge to go "argggg" and stomp an admirer into the pavement.

Get Out More Often. I am sooo a homebody. I love my home, so why should I have to leave it? Oh, yeah, I want to sell my work. A friend suggested that I do more public stuff, and pointed out that placing most or all of my public interactions on one reading or one public appearance per month can be stressful. I need practice. I need a guinea pig. How about you?

Get ready, World. "FrankenSteven" is coming to an interaction near you.

I Hate God

If you believe that you have a spirit or a soul, then you might also agree that most of your life you do not think about it. It's just there, and when you compare it with the needs and wants of the body, at times the soul seems to be non-existent. I do believe that I have a soul, mainly because I spent a great deal of my life trying to avoid thinking about it. It terrified me to think that inside of me was something that could be granted access to heaven (if I was good, and judged so) or sentenced to hell (if I were bad, and found guilty.) Complicating matters greatly was that I was a man who loved other men, and that everything I ever read or heard about men who loved men was that those who dared walk that path inherited a first-class, non-stop ticket to hell. A good reason if there was one to avoid thinking about souls.

Not that my soul was having it, because it did not. My mind is never still. From a very early age, I knew that I was a special sort of child. Every day, inside, my soul chattered away like a schoolboy, telling me to lift my head up and look at the boy looking at me from across the room, or to beware this particular alley because a rabid dog was waiting for me. I sometimes listened and took the advice, or ignored it and missed an opportunity for fun or suffered a bite. But it wasn't until I went to church that the voice was mute, and something else took over. Something not so good.

But first, a little history. Me and Christianity go way back. This is the part of the story that I know. My grandfather Steven, on my father's side, was a Baptist minister in rural Arkansas. His son Lucious became a Baptist minister as well, and now lives in Chicago. My own father sang with a short-lived gospel group called the Horns of Zion, and they toured parts of Michigan, Ohio, and Indiana. My mother was raised in a Lutheran church in Ohio, and was sometimes taken to a Baptist church by her grandmother, Buela. My mother raised us kids in a Lutheran church (my father refused to go for some reason), and it was there that I formally met the Father, the Son, and the Holy Ghost. I would have been better off not making their acquaintance. It was not an amiable relationship.

First, there was the venue: church. How could anybody stay awake in church? The purr of the minister's voice was a guaranteed snoozer. He'd read from his prepared sermon or the bible in a monotone that alternately made me want to laugh or sleep. Laughing was guaranteed to be rewarded with a slap from my mother; sleeping kept me quiet for fifteen minutes or so before she or my older sister would shake me awake. Outside of the church, I endured constant threats from God filtered through my mother about where bad little kids like me were likely to go. That coupled with what I thought were far too simplistic stories in bible class about sin, crowded my thoughts daily. These and other fucked up thoughts told me all I needed to know about God–He was judgmental, and didn't like little boys like me much.

And I didn't like Him. In fact I hated Him. What did he ever do for my family except provide a temporary reprieve from our miserable lives on Sunday mornings? My mother worked like a dog throughout my youth. My father had no less than two jobs his entire adult life, and still with their combined incomes struggled to raise five children. Understandably, my parents fought constantly about who was responsible for this or that. Did He step in and break it up? Or come with food when the refrigerator was empty? No.

God, as an entity, as an idea, did not work for me. When I got the courage, I let it go. The day it happened was like any other day for me. I was a rambunctious child with an opinion that I was willing to share with anyone in earshot. After becoming particularly sassy with my mother, she banished me from the kitchen and into my room. I only made it as far as the top of the stairs so that I could plan retaliation. Carefully, I sat there thinking of a way to get both her back and God back for punishing me. I patiently waited until my little brother Darryl came close enough to hear me before I uttered the words that would have a profound effect on my life forever.

"I hate God."

He didn't hear me at first, and asked me what I said. Once again, with perfect diction, I slowly walked the words out: "I-hate-GOD."

The plan worked beautifully. Darryl tore through the living room like an ambulance screaming "Awww!" and ran into the kitchen. I readied myself for the confrontation that never came. In her usual flippant fashion, my mother told my little brother, "Let him hate God, I don't care. Hate God all he wants. He's still on a punishment. Tell him that."

Next stop: Hell.

After I made that little declaration, my list of complaints against God mounted by the day. Picked on at school, at the park, at a friend's house. Not enough food, heat, or time to get up in the morning to go to school. My brother took my stuff, my older sisters were bossy and hogged the phone, and the younger one got any and everything she wanted just by crying for it. My clothing was old, raggedy, and out of style. Mom and daddy gave everybody but me everything. And what did God do? Not a thing. This God was sadistic. Praying seemed fairly useless, and so did acting like I believed that it worked. So I stopped.

That's when the spirits started visiting me. The first time it happened I thought it was a dream. The second time I wasn't so sure. The third time I was convinced that I was nuts. The encounter would normally start out with me in a semi-conscious state while lying on my bed or the couch. If I were on my bed, I would be facing the wall; if on the couch, I'd face the back of it.

The only way to describe what was happening to me is to liken the experience to listening to the noise that results from fumbling with the knobs on a transistor radio while trying to find a clear station. My whole body would be frozen while spirits roamed through my body, some talking, some crying or screaming. I never knew how long it would last, but while it was happening I would try to move my petrified limbs. First a finger, then a leg. Gradually, my lifeforce would again inhabit my limbs and allow me to move again. Scared, and terrified that it would happen to me again, I would sit up, dizzy with fear, and try to comprehend what had happened to me. I felt like a way station for wayward souls.

I remember telling myself that what was happening was ridiculous. I didn't believe in God. Did that automatically mean I was going hell? And if so, were demons periodically hanging out in my body? And I was already poor, so, like, could God or Satan go pick on someone who was better off? I offered up this prayer to whatever entity was listening. "Leave me alone, at least until I get myself together."

The incidents/visits stopped, and so did my anger towards God. Surely, it had to be God with whom I had brokered the deal. Still, a nagging sense inside told me that I just faked myself out to get a little breathing room. That a raging puberty and insurgent sexuality almost immediately filled the little opening that either God or I made for myself. Overwhelmed and incessantly horny, I decided to try to be a good Christian and go to church.

Once again in church, I sat alone, without my mother or siblings. The pews were brown, cool, and slick under my pants. I carried a bible that I got from a thrift store. The pastor I knew as a child, a white man, had retired, and now another younger white minister stood in the pulpit. Everything was basically the same: the monotone lecture, the red hymnal books secure on the shelf in front of me, the alert faces of the adults, the anxious or sleeping faces of the children or elders. This time, however, I listened with a matured ear. I was 20, had my own apartment, and was in complete denial of my sexuality. The thought that someone might discover that I was homosexual terrified me so, hence my trying to wash it away with a weekly trip to the church.

But it didn't work. The ascent of my consciously acting on my desires for other men was directly proportionate to my waning interest in attending church. Though I stopped, I was still interested in God, or better put, matters of the spirits. As I made my way through college, I wrote poetry that started to question more than the existence of God; the poems became a way to dialogue about the ways in which spirituality manifested itself. Godstuff was my preoccupation for a number of years, until one day I had a dream that not only confirmed for me the existence of God, but also clarified that what I had been doing all along was looking for a dragon.

Next: The Resurrection

I was in the backyard of my parents' home. It was dawn, and spring was busily breaking up the ice. Mud and water commingled at my feet. I looked up in the sky. Frozen in a block of ice was a dragon upside down, floating in the air high above me. The ice was rapidly melting, and I feared that the dragon would fall on my head. The block actually floated a few feet away from me, where the dragon dropped out from the now completely melted block of ice and into a neighbor's backyard. It came towards me. Suddenly, I was looking out of my bedroom window watching the dragon follow me around the house while my father followed the dragon. I didn't feel like I was being chased, nor did I feel that my father was chasing or hunting the dragon.

Freaked but not scared, I related the dream to a co-worker the next day. She was shocked. Rolita, a budding spiritualist and all-around good woman, and I talked about the significance of the dragon in Chinese cultures, and how the dragon represents feminine energy. She gave me a copy of the book Jambalaya by Luisah Teish. It changed my life.

Jambalaya chronicles Teish's development as a Yoruba priestess in the Oshun tradition. The book provided a brief history of Ifa, and how it consecrated with Christianity and formed, among other things, voodoo and hoodoo, and a whole mess of things. Teish's personal narrative helped me to get closer to the idea of Ifa, and I read everything I could about it, voodoo and hoodoo. Orishas (representatives of energy in the

Yoruba pantheon of spirituality) by the hundreds. I felt close to
these ideas of the spirit. Teish recounted stories similar to my
own. She laughed and told great stories about healing and
growing and finding her spirit. Who knew that religion could
be so much fun?

For once, spirituality began to make some sense to me,
particularly the Orisha named Ellegua. After Ollodumare (God),
the next most powerful being is Ellegua, the divine messenger.
Ellegua is the deity who removes obstacles and opens the paths,
doors, and roads of opportunity and success for humans. He
also takes the prayers of humans to the Orishas, and acts as a
conduit for their energies. Without him, no ceremony can be
done nor can spiritual work be fully realized. Hmmm. What I
found most intriguing about Ellegua is his energy, which is seen
as mischievous and playful. Throughout my life I have enjoyed
joking or pulling the rug out from under people, literally and
figuratively.

So bring on de fun!

Ultimately, I didn't (and won't) join any group or any
religion (who needs an intermediary? I can talk to God myself!),
but if I had to choose one it would be Ifa. My exploration in
this religion led me down a much more familiar spiritual road,
one where I didn't have to stop being me–the rambunctious me,
the one I like being–to be right with God. Ifa was a good
introduction to the different ways that one could experience the
spirit with many names and various manifestations. This was a
relief to me. I even stopped hating God. It could all work, you
know?

See, before there was Eshu, there was Jesus, and before
there was Jesus, there was God, and He said unto me: boy, you
better get right with God. And I did. By getting right with me.

If I Should Die Tonight: Instructions for the Living from the Newly Dead

Ah, no more getting up in the morning to brush my teeth or make my bed. No more laundry. No more news that isn't news. No more listening to another paid-for politician or some apathetic soul sitting on her ass. No more jealousy, no more coveting my neighbor's ass. No more taking in and disseminating gossip. No more washing dishes. No more feeling guilty about anything. No more wishing I had more. No more conversations with emotionally disturbed men. No more fucking commercials with smiling, shining waifish creatures from outer space. No more trying to impress anybody. No more watching people yearn for what they didn't have as a child. No more trying to figure out why.

Death: the perfect antidote to living.

I am going to die, like everybody else, and I have no idea when or where or how. But, like all Capricorns on their shit, I do have a few instructions in that eventuality.

There is a packet on my desk containing a photo that is to be my official death photo. I don't want to be peeking over from the Afterlife and see that some lousy-assed mugshot is the last visual my family, friends, and admirers will see. Use this photo in the obituary and any forthcoming volumes of posthumously published work, and any "remembering our beloved Steven" tributes.

As for the wake, funeral, or whatever: It is my wish to be cremated and to have my ashes thrown in the Atlantic Ocean. Or the Pacific Ocean. Or any ocean, just not the Great Lakes. They are not so great to me! If, for some reason, I cannot be cremated, then drop my rotting corpse in a pine box. Do not embalm me! I want to return to the Earth post haste!

Now, here's a tough request, but one that I think you will come to agree with, once you think about it. At any remembrance service, don't extol my great virtue. Everyone knows all the great shit I did anyway, so why bore them? Try something different when you get to the podium. Rank on my ass. Talk about how selfish I was. How I thought I was all that and a bag of crab cakes. Talk about my rampant promiscuity. My stanking attitude. How I could never cut my mustache straight. Or that once I got tired of you, you were toast. Talk about how I thought I was a one-man cultural revolution. Or that I was a bastard.

Roast me. Don't yap about my writing. We all know it changed countless lives. Who doesn't know that? Talk about my bland cooking. My receding hairline. My fat head. How my second toe is larger than my first one. Talk about my one testicle. Stuff like that. Conversation starters.

I will be watching. If any of you, particularly those who do not know me, think you're gonna get to go on about what a great guy I was, mark my words, I will get you. Think of me as the monster under your bed, or the low, creepy moan in your closet. I will be the zit that appears on your face the day before you take that important photo. I will cause all kinds of chaos in your pathetic life because I can. I'm dead and you cannot catch me!

Unless of course, you die too.

Momma's Little Baby Loves
Shortening Names

Most folks have no idea what the hell is going on in the world today. Most. They believe everything they read and hear, and do little in the way of integrating experiential and learned knowledge. Most people just want to go along to get along. It is, I believe, what keeps people stuck in their pathetic lives.

Except you, of course, right?

Yeah reader, you always know *exactly* what's going on, don't you? The down low, ipso factos. Nothing gets past your radar, huh?

Wrong! You're up on things like a cat on an ice-cold roof! You have no idea what's going on in the world, let alone in your own city! You think that Africa is a country. You believe that America has your best interests at heart! You think after a night after boozing it up that you are one sexy babe, that no one could resist you. Generally you think you are hot stuff.

Guess what? You're not. You never were. You'll never be. You have the IQ of a rock—scratch that, you're not that creative or interesting. You are a scourge, you lousy-assed excuse for a carbon-based life form.

You...shorten...names.

What kind of moron upon being introduced to someone decides right then and there, to shorten their name? Think about it?

Read:

"Hey, how are you, my name is Bob," you say.

"Bob, my name is Steven."

"STEVE, I'M GLAD TO MEET YOU!"

Steve, I'm glad to meet you? Who the hell is Steve? Was he standing behind me? Does Steven sound like Steve? Help me out here.

I wake bathed in sweat. Covers all tangled about my feet. Visions of Steves jitterbug in my head. What kind of world do we live in? I live with having my name shortened every day of my life! Hacked to bits. Slaughtered like a pig. Do you know what that's like?

And it only gets worse.

Try to explain to someone that your name is ___ and they look at you like, what's your problem? My problem, jerk ass, is that you ain't saying my name! And I am one of the lucky ones. Someone with a non-English name has to listen to all kinds of butchered versions of their name daily, sometime hourly. Some just give in and say call me Kim or Sam. Me, I am not so ready to concede. These bastards must be stopped!

I lived in Atlanta for two years. Steve this, Steve that. And a few Mookie's and Boo's tossed in to make me totally nuts. And all those Buppies. I am scarred for life.

Only a few people I know actually sympathize with my plight. Most people want to belong, and so do I. But when I leave a room, I want to take my name with me, not Steve. And I don't care if I am liked or not, nanny, nanny poo poo!

Know what I think? This "Steve" character is a helluva lot nicer than me. He laughs at everybody's jokes. He likes sports. He roars when his team scores and throws his popcorn up in the air. He thinks he is just fine and dandy. He has no shame.

So you see the dilemma. Or can you? Oh, that's right, you are probably an offender. Can't see the "Steven" for the "Steve"? Youthinks I protest too much? That shortening names displays a want for intimacy, a yearning to identify, a genuine belief that different people can get along just by dropping a few letters from your name? Phooey.

That's exactly my point. How in the hell are we really gonna get along if we don't even want to call each other by our real names? I watch people struggle with names that sound foreign and I am always amazed at how often they look at the person as if he or she had a problem. Like taking two extra seconds to learn someone's name is a problem. The problem is that people aren't, by nature, tolerant, and/or interested in anything that ain't familiar. We are not the world. What we often are is a bunch of people who want to be treated with respect, but not be respectful.

I don't mind learning your name, becoming a part of your world. But when you don't want to even call me by my name, that's when we have problems. So don't shorten names—or at least, my name anyway. Call me what I call myself (on a good day) and you and I will get along just fine. And I guarantee that your life will vastly improve.

Muscles Crowd My Mind

To have muscles or not to have muscles. That is the question.

I tell people that I work out to take care of my body, but what I really want is to be big, muscular and strong so that I can punch the faces of all the jerks who hurt and taunted me in school when I was a kid! Yeah!

Whew. That was a relief. *Give them the nutty thoughts first, Steven, go ahead, there you go, ah.* Being a slim Jim all my life has had its up and downs, and I want to share a few of those experiences in this essay because, well, I feel like talking about it.

But first let me give you some context for my recent musings on the state of my body. Recently I went vegetarian, and in the following month I couldn't conceive of going into the gym and doing my regular routine. No shit. I was terrified. I think: no animal products means lesser or no strength. I would think this lying in the bed fetal-like with my thumb in my mouth. My energy level has subsided. My worse nightmare is being at the gym and dropping 300 lbs. on my head.

Added to that are these contradictory thoughts I have about my body image. You know, what I said earlier about knocking people upside the head and then kissing my muscles, that sort of thing. I want to look good so that the boys and girls will slobber. But more than anything, I want to appear like it's not hard at all, you know, working out like an athlete, just bouncing and bulging down the street full of life in tight jeans. Yeah, I am seeing a therapist.

Yes, all of these and other thoughts are connected to my being black and a manhandler. Well, more so being a manhandler. I think I have the black part down. I just am. But being black and a manhandler in this society is work, let me tell you. Just when you think you get a leg up and proudly declare, "I'm black and I love other men sexually and I love it!," there are other things to consider, like YOUR FUCKING LOOKS!

I hate my vanity. It keeps me in the mirror gazing into my own eyes far too much. A pimple can exhaust my self-esteem. My hair, once bushy and bright, has decided that it will now grow when and where it wants to. I have tried talking to my hair, but it just ain't coming out no more. It has retired. So, of course I have to cut my hair, oh, let's say EVERY FUCKING WEEK so that I can afford to think of something other than A) getting older, B) getting older, or C) you guessed it, wrinkling up and dying.

To be desirable (and maybe I have this all wrong; you tell me) the first thing anybody notices is your looks. A relatively attractive appearance is key to your market value on the street. The more muscular and "handsome" one is, the more options for dick. On a good day, I might have one muscle or two. Having cream-colored skin in black America (shit, all over the world!) is always a plus, except when it's all that's expected of me.

From what I've heard and witnessed, it's all-good if your dick swings past your knees. Having a large dick is like having a free credit card. You can charge, charge, charge! Being endowed is self-confidence. Many a brother I know (biblically) has expected some congratulations or cash reward for having a long dong. So a word of advice: advertise appropriately, guys. If there's an occasion to flaunt your stuff, do it! The tighter the pants, the better. If the requests don't come pouring in like you want, there's always porno. It's always looking for, pardon the pun, fresh meat. My dick is six inches long. I measured it when I was in my 20s. And again in my thirties just to see if it had grown. It didn't.

Being young can circumvent the previous two attributes. Youth is its own reward. You're fresh, full of life, and have the image of being new. We live in a youth-oriented culture, and everything young is wonderful, so how can you lose? When I was in my twenties, things seemed possible to me in a way they aren't now. Granted, my self-esteem was shot most of the time, but I felt freer, more ambitious and full of energy. Now, in my 38th year, I'm concerned about my diet because of all the fucked up diseases you can get just by eating anything and everything. My energy level is still high, but I crash and burn a lot more often because I haven't learned the fine art of relaxation.

So let's backtrack a moment about my muscles. Man, let me tell you, if there weren't all those damn weights and exercise rooms at the gym, well, I'd be there every day! I'd be sucking down all kinds of steroids to get the muscles I so dearly thought would make my life so much better as a youngster and card-carrying member of the man loving man community. Oh, just the thought of having big muscles delights me! Can you picture it? Everyone would be like, oooo-wee? Look at Steven's muscles! I'd buy nothing but tight shirts and pants! And, of course, I'd act like I was the same old guy. Behind closed doors, I'd be kissing my muscles.

So here I am at gym on the regular and I like it. I try hard and I get results. But I wonder if the two muscles I have now will ultimately make me an asshole. There's a lot of evidence to suggest this eventuality. Go to Any Gym USA where many a muscle bound guy works out and, trust me, they ain't working out with dictionaries. They also tend to lay it on thick with answers to questions you didn't even ask. "Lift this way, put more weight on, keep your stomach in." Keep my stomach in? Motherfucker, that's why I am here, I can't keep my stomach in.

I think my saving grace is that I do take some pride in not doing the same thing to others that I feel was done to me: treat them like shit because they don't measure up to my, well, no everyone's standard of beauty. Everyone has worth. And even though I believe this I am still compelled to run to the gym in the morning and work my muscles, so you can see how beautiful I am.

Cuz now I have three, count 'em, three muscles.

Stop My Libido, I Want To Get Off!

Yo, when I signed up to be gay, I had no idea that meant I'd stay perpetually horny. Since the age of ten, I have had an erection the size of Texas floating about in my gabardines. A gust of wind can set me off. A pretty smile can make it dance. Memories moisten my member.

Think I'm kidding? Wish I were. I am a shade off from being a sex addict, and the only thing separating me from that state of being is that I am a crabby, persnickety bastard who will and can not fuck just any man. I can go without sex for months (minus masturbation) without losing my mind or composure. As of late, I can't even keep a fuck buddy around, mainly because no applicants have stepped up to the plate and besides, I'm busy. But I can't lie. If I were really interested in getting a regular booty call going on, I'd have to hold interviews.

"So, it says here that you like to cuddle, is that right?" I say, as I glance at his application, and peer at him over the top of my glasses which sit on the tip of my nose.

"Yeah, I do, right after sex," says the guy. "I like it. I think it's a good thing."

"We'll give you a call. Tell the next applicant to come in backwards. Naked."

Next guy walks in backward. Naked. This is a good start.

"Uh, why am I here?" he says, with his back to me.

"You're here to interview to be my booty call."

"What's a booty call?"

"You're hired."

Sometimes, sex is just sex, and that's all, nothing more. A way to clean out that backed-up energy. If I want to cuddle, I'll call a friend, someone who has no interest in being with me whatsoever and we'll watch a movie. When and if I enter boyfriend/lover land again, cuddling will be fine if I don't have my habits on that evening, and would rather sleep alone.

Let me talk for a minute about what is commonly referred to as the "booty call." I remember that, not too long ago, booty calls were about sex. Now there seem to be all kinds of conditions, like, God forbid, staying the night. When did this get written into the contract? Leave, leave, get thy underpants and leave! No doubt it should be an option, but with some brothers, the sex is all they have to offer, and all they want to give. That's just fine.

Sex is an activity, a sport, a way to find out if all the parts are in order. My twenties were a haze-filled ménage of experimental, outrageous, wild and sometimes dangerous sex. I had boyfriends. I had other people's boyfriends. I had a husband, who, at the time, was still married. I had so much sex from 1984 to 1994 that, by right, I should be sated for the rest of my life, but that is not the case. At this point, I think I've given up on a male companion, and settled for parts. I think God made me like men in order to keep the population down, because back then I could have (and still can) populate a small planet by sundown. I would be several baby's daddies.

I know I'm supposed to talk about sex in this essay, but what lies underneath, at least for me in some respects, is a deep yearning to be totally loved. And I haven't found a guy who has filled my heart in awhile. So bring on the booty.

When did this start? Early on as a kid, when looking at boob magazines, masturbation and copping a feel from the neighborhood girls (and sometimes boys) were daily things to do. When my teens hit, I was absolutely under the power of my lust. It would call me like a mad hypnotist. "Steven, come here," it would say. "Yes, master," I'd reply with eyes spinning like tops. "Find the booty," "Yes, master!"

Dealing with lust as a man on his way to forty is another something altogether. Who has time for all that? I don't. The older I get, the less interested I become in the meat market...have the energy to haul it up and make it look cute for anybody. That's not to say that I am ready to settle down like some regular yokel; all it means is that I believe I can control my ding dong urges a little bit easier. In fact, things are working out kinda dandy. I'm relaxed and taking a lot more walks now. It's people like Samuel Delany, however, who worry me.

I love this man. He lets me call him Chip. Okay, so he lets a lot of people call him Chip, but that's not the point. The point is that I think he's had more sex than everyone in Texas, and you know they have nothing better to do than fuck. And he's frank about it, read his books. So anyways, I'm talking to my bestest friend Chip one morning and he offered up some pretty bad news. This elder, this man of letters, this gentleman, scholar, and benevolent spirit, told me that not only will my body parts go the way of the crapper, but that my libido will probably stay the same. Maybe even increase. Oh joy.

I hope he's wrong. I mean I love sex and all, but I was looking forward to a nice relaxing day in the sun, drinking lemonade and…well, you know the corny rest.

The Woman in Me

"Welcome to oppression."

I was wobbling down, no, clip-clopping down three flights of stairs to show Elspeth, the director of <u>Blue Nails,</u> an experimental film with a narrative about the mixed-up issue that is miscegenation, that I could indeed walk in heels. What a sight to behold. All made up and somewhere to hoe. But I could walk in heels. No ankle-bending bumbling here.

Cast as a woman named "Zoe," I was prancing about in a poofy wig and dress and high heels for about four weeks. My transformation into "Zoe," a mulluta leaning toward high drama and low self-esteem, was interesting. I am a debutante sashaying about in a fluffy, shiny, pink prom dress with a five o'clock shadow. RuPaul I ain't. More like BooPaul.

When I first auditioned for the part, I was pretty sad. Didn't think I would be cast as anything, but I was shocked when the director offered me the role, as a "woman." We all had a good laugh. I am an okay looking guy, but as a woman, I looked as if I was beat with an ugly stick. Still I was up for the challenge, but it really didn't sink in that I would be in full drag until I was on the set, under hot lights being made up and sternly instructed not to smear my makeup. Smear my makeup? Hee-larious. There I was, sitting in a chair, memorizing my lines while my cheeks were being patted down with powder. Funny. What a life.

My role called for a 50's housewifey type. What does a woman in the 50's act like? Donna Reed or Etta James? Director says Donna Reed. My scene is based on a sitcom. I play a woman as a man who's not exactly a drag queen. It's pretty complicated.

In costume (dress), I am delicate, soft, and calm. I cry at the drop of a hat that Bobby or Jimmy didn't call. I flounce down on a bed. I break into song about ever lasting love. Other than that, there's not much going on in my head. Lalalalalalalala.

Kaye, the costume designer, fitted me for my dress. Wow. What a fucked up experience. This little beauty caused trouble the minute she took it off the rack. I put my arm in the neck and stood triumphantly. What I needed, and thanks to Kaye, got it, was a dress spotter, someone to place the monstrosity of lace and taffeta over my head while I stood there like a football referee screaming "score!" When I finally got the damn thing on, I was given a bustier with padding to give me a nice pointy set of boobs. After I finished feeling myself up, I pondered over how cumbersome women's clothes are. Put that here, put that there. Yuk, yuk.

"Now," Kaye instructed, "I want you to pay close attention so you'll know how to do this on your own." I nodded, but I wasn't sure I wanted to know how to do it myself. "You'll need to put on this (I forgot the name; it's like a slip but they make a dress big and poofy underneath–petticoat!) before you put on the dress so things don't slide underneath." Please, it's all sliding underneath, I think. The only things that aren't sliding about are my shoes and stockings.

Shoes and stockings. Tight-assed shoes and knee-high stockings. The stockings aren't so bad. Women wear this stuff all the time, right? Fuck, Prince the Munchkin has done splits in heels a lot higher than my patent leather dandies. When I was told to go get a pair of fuck-me black pumps from wardrobe, all I could think about were naked women in Penthouse and Playboy Magazine. Naked white women bending over tables or on their backs with a suggestive finger playing about their juicy red lips. The inference is that these women are so eager to fuck you that they forget to take off their shoes. I dunno.

I'm walking to and fro, trying to impress the other actors, but all I get are giggles. The director shoots me many "women don't act like that" looks. I am told to stand up straight, push my pelvis back and stick my chest out. I look and feel like a chicken–a sexy chicken, but a chicken nonetheless.

Before I call it a day, one of my fellow actors comments on how great my feet look. "It's the stockings," I told her, and then remember how I liked the look of smoothy feet. How soft. Wow. I grabbed my heels and made a hasty retreat.

The shooting went well, but I was nervous. Walking and talking and flouncing about can take it out of you. And yes, I am one ugmo of a woman. I wouldn't even date me.

You're Gonna Be Sooo Disappointed:
To all Present and Future Stevenites

Your work means so much to me.

I think you are amazing.

I just can't wait to meet you.

Are you God?

The answer is "yes" to the last question, but that's another story.

These are samples of the things people have said to me since I started making my business pubic, I mean, public, that is, publishing. One essay in particular, "I Was a Teenage Sissy…and I Still Am," hit hard and resonated with a lot of people, and not just skinny-assed, mealy-mouthed, all-around prissy punks like yours truly. Mothers and fathers wrote to me, praising me for my honesty, sometimes asking for advice on how to protect their children from the bullshit I experienced. Just love them, I'd say—and never send them to school!

But the majority of the folk who sent me e-mails were brothers like myself, who were beat up to be beat down, boys endeavoring to become "like that" men who were grappling with the effects of homophobia, delivered all too often at the hands of our relatives and loved ones.

Many of those men who were brave enough to reach out to me were erudite, candid, and warm. An e-mail exchange with a Japanese artist resulted in tipping the balance in his decision to relocate to the Big Apple and my gaining a new friend. I even got a few admirers of my work, folks I call "Stevenites," (thanks, Herukhuti—he coined the term) people who like my writing, some who have been fortunate to gaze upon His Majesty in all his yellow splendor. While fun for the ego, it can be irritating sometimes (like, what do you say to a person ga-ga over you?), but mostly it's just plain fascinating. Getting attention for simply scribbling down my thoughts? Me, getting laid over a few

paragraphs? Me, who finds humor in things that I am certain
would get my passport snatched, being praised? Woo-hoo!
Writing is for me.

While I'll admit having been an "ite" in my life for countless
writers (Toni Morrison, James Baldwin, Yukio Mishima),
musicians (Prince, Tori Amos), and lunch ladies (who shall
remain nameless), I think being given attention for something
that I like to do, have to do, am still learning to do, is surreal.
Like, who the fuck is Steven G. Fullwood anyway? I'll tell you
who. He's a sweet high yella nigra boy from Toledo, Ohio
(that's round on the sides and HI in the middle!). I'm so damned
light I shock myself when I look in the mirror! I'm the smart
aleck kid who never grew up and never wants to.

But enough of the jokes and back to the business of the
word, word? When I write my name I am pleased with it.
Steven G. Fullwood: two syllables, one syllable, and then two
more syllables...very literary, if you ask me. It's always a kick in
the pants to see my by-line until my beady little eyes catch a
mistake, misspelling or typo throbbing like a toothache in the
middle of one of my carefully crafted sentences. Then my
stomach flops a bit, and I throw myself on the ground because I
know millions of people (okay, maybe three people) will read
my mistake(s) and shake their heads in disgust. What a rotten
writer this guy is, they'll say. After bingeing on ecstasy and
heroin, I will find the strength to shake my fist at the sky, like
Job, to curse the day I was born. Me, a five-syllable loser!

One small fact: What I love to see—and I admit it's
perverse—is, when meeting an eager "Stevenite," his facial
expression slowly morphing from very excited, to just excited,
to not-so excited, to plain disappointment. At a conference I
recently attended, some guy with a screwed-up face told me
that I shouldn't have cut my hair, inferring that I was cuter with
locks. Well fuck you, ugly jerk, but keep reading my writing,
please? Another guy at another conference gushed profusely
and then just stood in front of me until I ran out of "thank you's"
and "I appreciate that's," "thank you, I appreciate that's," and

"freshen your drink, Gov'ner's?" After a few minutes of dead air, the Steven G. Fullwood show had indeed ended, and he walked away. Maybe I should have offered him some dick.

What I expect from readers is very little: read my words. What readers expect, however, from me is a performance, which is reasonable while I am at the podium or table or running a workshop, but sucks the dog when I am Joe Regular after the show. Look, like most people, I like attention, but I am a writer, not a magician, and there is no rabbit coming out of my hat. Writing can be a very, very boring exercise. I do it because I like expressing myself this way. And while I am my writing, I am not only my writing. That is, I am some guy plunking out the words in my room, hopefully making some kind of sense in order to engage someone other than myself. I am curious about what it is I think. I write for myself.

But just so that we are all clear about the man and the writer, let me give all you hopefuls a leg up on the differences between the two.

The writer is a welcoming communicator with his arms open, while the man is moody and runs in fear, arms extended, from a ringing phone.

The writer is relaxed and engaging. The man is a twisted nerve ending, fraying, hoping the audience doesn't see his mismatched socks and beat-up shoes.

The writer is neat and composed. The man is a belly-scratching oaf who cannot seem to cut his mustache straight to save his life, so that's why he doesn't wear one.

The writer looks great on paper; you might think he's attractive. The man's got a pimple, can you see it, I know you can because, jeez, there it is and it's so big and why on this day of all days do I have a big-assed juicy pimple protruding from my head like a baby nipple, God, I hate this day, aaaarrrrg!

The writer smiles at you and holds your hand from sentence to sentence. The man will push you down to the ground and treat you like the dirtbag you are, dirtbag!

The writer has concerns for all humankind. The man wants

the organizer of the reading dead because he fucked up his check by misspelling his name "Tullwood," and now he has to beg his landlord for another two weeks until a new check is cut.

The writer is believes in people; it is the reason why he writes. The man is confident that most people are Satan's spawn and have little in the way of contributing to the well-being of the world other than offering up a little back and front for his sssssssweeet sausage.

Oh yes, the man is a pisser.

But dear reader, do not fear. I am writing to you from the recesses of my heart, engaging you in a narrative form where I hope to make it clear that we all can live together and discover and revel in everyone's unique talents and create a world beyond all of our expectations—free of war, of pestilence, and of fear. But until that day comes, I'll be in the back, tearing up some fresh Stevenite booty, so don't disturb me, aiight?

EPILOGUE

An Expatriate Speaks

Dear Toledo,

Excuse my late reply (several years), but I had to give myself a few years to think about why I left your sorry ass. This letter was written with all the hope that it will clear up any misconception or confusion about why I packed my glad rags and got the hell away from you.

If you've read through this book and the essays, it should be apparent why someone like me couldn't be with someone like you. Sure, you were good to me during the first years of my life. Running down the street, climbing trees, hanging with my friends, playing tag and hide and go-get-it, and learning to learn. These were some good times.

But then I grew up and I wanted to leave you. Why? Oh, you know why. You couldn't love someone like me, really, and I loathed you. I thought you sucked big time. What did you offer me? Excuses for a good life when the only thing you offered were basically four things: movies, and places to shop and eat, and bowl. Occasionally there was a concert, maybe a cultural event or two. Overall, I felt culturally deprived; I read the Village Voice and Rolling Stone, pondering a life outside of what I saw as prison gates.

There are many memories of you dancing in my head. Your imprint is on everything I do—my manner, my smile, and my vision. Indeed, you are in my blood. When your name is mentioned now, or when someone asks where I came from, all I think about are the reasons why I left you. You made me sick. But I was scared to leave you, scared to even board the plane. Then one day something happened that changed my life forever—my best friend Carla got a scholarship to Columbia University, and since I didn't want to live in New York initially, I didn't pack my bags. Get this: she was going to leave me in your rotten clutches!

She made her announcement, and I was stunned. I sure as hell was not staying with you without her. So I made a way to leave. I conjured up a scholarship at Clark Atlanta University, and in the first four frosty days of 1996, I spread my wings–just me and my Toyota down, down, down to the first place I would ever live, several states away from you. And I was free.

Well, Toledo, you tried to appease me. There was my family, who I love and cherish. You were centrally located; leaving you for a weekend was always good. Chicago, four hours; Cleveland, an hour and a half; Detroit and Ann Arbor, 45 minutes. And you gave me many wonderful, selfless friends who helped me tolerate your abuse for the first 29 years of my life. Which, in most cases, would be enough, but I had other plans, ones that I didn't even know about. And, of course, the price I had to pay to stay with you was enormous.

In exchange for my creativity and intelligence, you offered me a manager's position at one of your libraries.

HahahahahahahahahahahahahaHAHAHAHAHAHAHAH AHAHAHAHAHAHAHAHAHAHAHAHAHAHAHAHAHAHAHA HAHAHAHAHAHAHAHAHAHAHAHAHAHAHAHAHAHAHAH AHAHAHAHAHAHAHAHAHAHAHAHAHAHAHAHAHAHAHA HAHAHAHAHAHAHAHAHAHAHAHAHAHAHAHAHAHAHAH AHAHAHAHAHAHAHAHAHAHAHAHAHAHAHAHAHAHAHA HAHAHA HAHAHAHAHAHAHA.

My father, a man who has never worked less than two jobs his entire adult life, in addition to most black people born before or around 1940, thought that the offer was a good deal. "You got a good job," was/is a popular line and often refers to a black person who has a government or factory job. One had security. All I can imagine is that, had I stayed, I would have shriveled a little each day until there was no more of me.

Toledo, you laid out the days before me, and they seemed to have no end. You had no place in my dreams. You demanded that I be "normal" in an environment rife with racism, homophobia, economic despair, rampant violence, and, good God, boredom! I could forgive the first four, but, jeez, you offered nothing in the way of cultural activities. Your local papers suck, your television stations are corny, and last time, I was there the only independent film theatre had been closed for nearly a decade. How was I supposed to be fed? Concerts were few, unless you liked gospel music and chitlin' circuit plays. Sports events were plentiful, but as an adult, must I be a fan of high school sports? Psst, please.

When I was a kid, I always dreamed of living somewhere else, not because the hood itself was so terrible, but because it simply wasn't my lifestyle of choice. Baby, I have to travel the world! It's mine! I have to be with people who are like me: fearless, conscious, educated, eccentric, and, in some cases, back diggers. Yeah, I know you don't know what that means, but that is why I can't be with you. That said, you should not feel any sadness about my leaving you because I only had two choices: leave or stay–or better put, live or die.

I chose to live. Let me state for the record that I do not hate you, Toledo. I can actually say that I love you, but from a distance. You taught me a lot. You taught me to find me.

Before I realized how valuable you were, I focused only on your negative qualities. It used to be this horrible thing in my head, you know, being from a place that is home and feeling homeless. I knew deep in my heart that you were not my home, at least as an adult. Do you know what it is like to feel "homeless?" To feel that your birthplace failed you? I did. I carried those fucked up feelings around with me for the longest. I don't feel that way any longer, because I realize that although you are not the place for me to live you helped shape the boy who ran down your streets and climbed your trees. Thank you. You watched me hang with my friends while we played tag and hide and go-get-it. Thank you. You watched me as I learned to learn. For that I am eternally grateful. Toledo, you prepared me for the world. It was only when I left you that I realized that not only did I have to leave you, but that I had a long way to go if I wanted to be happy, healthy and responsible for the needs of my soul.

While growing up, I was witness to the death of many dreams of family members and friends. Rather than making me cautious, those beat-down folk fueled my desire not to become just another person who said he or she wanted to do this or that and was just talking out the side of his or her neck. Lacking education, lacking focus, scared, or just plain unlucky, it didn't matter to me. From day one, I knew I was different and that whatever stopped other Toledoans would not, could not, stop me. I figured I could either decry my lack of opportunities, or I could make them. That's what I did for myself; I created opportunities. And I thank you for getting me started: the boy you saw running down the street, climbing trees, hanging with his friends, playing tag and hide and go-get-it, and learning to learn.

ABOUT THE AUTHOR

Steven G. Fullwood is a writer currently living in Harlem.